STRATEGIC
Reading Groups

Companion Website Available

STRATEGIC
Reading Groups
Guiding Readers in the Middle Grades

Jennifer Berne
Sophie C. Degener

Foreword by Donna Ogle

CORWIN
A SAGE Company

CORWIN
A SAGE Company

FOR INFORMATION

Corwin
A SAGE Company
2455 Teller Road
Thousand Oaks, California 91320
(800) 233-9936
Fax: (800) 417-2466
www.corwin.com

SAGE Publications Ltd.
1 Oliver's Yard
55 City Road
London, EC1Y 1SP
United Kingdom

SAGE Publications India Pvt. Ltd.
B 1/I 1 Mohan Cooperative Industrial Area
Mathura Road, New Delhi
India 110 044

SAGE Publications Asia-Pacific Pte. Ltd.
3 Church Street
#10-04 Samsung Hub
Singapore 049483

Acquisitions Editor: Carol Chambers Collins
Associate Editor: Megan Bedell
Editorial Assistant: Sarah Bartlett
Production Editor: Cassandra Margaret Seibel
Copy Editor: Gretchen Treadwell
Typesetter: Hurix Systems Pvt. Ltd.
Proofreader: Theresa Kay
Indexer: Jean Casalegno
Cover Designer: Karine Hovsepian
Permissions Editor: Karen Ehrmann

Printed in the United States of America

Library of Congress Cataloging-in-Publication Data

Berne, Jennifer.
Strategic reading groups : guiding readers in the middle grades / Jennifer Berne and Sophie C. Degener ; foreword by Donna Ogle.
p. cm.
Includes bibliographical references and index.
ISBN 978-1-4522-0286-0 (pbk.)
1. Reading (Middle school) 2. Group reading.
I. Degener, Sophie. II. Title.
LB1632.B485 2012
428.4071'2—dc23
2011039688

This book is printed on acid-free paper.

MIX
Paper from responsible sources
FSC
www.fsc.org
FSC® C014174

12 13 14 15 16 10 9 8 7 6 5 4 3 2 1

Contents

Additional materials and resources related to *Strategic Reading Groups: Guiding Readers in the Middle Grades* can be found at www.corwin.com/strategicreadinggroups.

List of Online Resources

Foreword

What a timely guide to comprehension development by Jennifer Berne and Sophie Degener. The importance of developing students' comprehension of challenging texts is clear in this era of Common Core State Standards (CCSS). Berne and Degener provide a well-conceived path to strategic reading development using informational texts. They show concretely how teachers can identify and address comprehension issues for capable as well as more challenged readers. The specific focus of this intervention is to identify each student's reading abilities and then guide them in becoming more strategic. It is like all good coaching; the coach first watches and listens to the student's performance and then identifies one or two areas for focused attention so they can improve. While that may seem simple, providing such instruction has been a challenge for teachers because there is such a range of abilities in any class and many readers don't evidence problems with the assigned readings. It has also been a challenge because many teachers don't feel confident in coaching students to higher levels of reading performance. In this book, Berne and Degener lay out in detail ways teachers can quickly identify students' current strategies and coach them in using more advanced or appropriate ones. The multiple examples of dialogues between students and teachers provide wonderful models for teachers to follow.

It is always special to be invited into the development process of careful literacy educators. Berne and Degener share how their design for middle grade strategic reading has been developed during their current work with teachers. Their suggestions throughout reflect their sensitivity to teachers' contexts, questions, and constraints. As I read the text I was amazed at how they regularly addressed key issues teachers need to have resolved before they will alter their instruction. The clear distinction they make between teaching literature and strategic reading is important; too often, middle grade teachers have focused only on teaching with quality literature. Now, with the CCSS insistence on a balance between reading literature and reading informational texts, this model provides a clear roadmap for teachers and schools. It also helps remind teachers that all students need to read challenging texts to keep moving forward in their literacy so they can be confident in reading the increasingly wide range of materials and text formats expected in this information-rich era. Another issue regularly raised by teachers is how to find time to do everything asked of them. Berne and Degener address this issue directly by providing possible schedules for reading and language arts instruction so time can be allotted for strategic reading groups with one-to-one coaching.

As I read the text I was also reminded of how important it is that teachers find ways to hear each of their students read orally. During my graduate studies I received a call from the local high school English chair. She explained that while substituting in a junior level English course she had spotted a young man who was clearly a nonreader. She wanted me to tutor him—which I subsequently did. How much better it would have been if Claude and similar students could have been identified much earlier; the longer their lack of reading skill persists the more they suffer. The pain of not reading well is a huge burden many students carry. Students won't be able to hide their lack of reading abilities if middle grade teachers regularly listen to their students read orally and guide their strategic reading development. That's one of the great gifts of this book; it provides teachers clear directions and multiple examples of how they can include regular monitoring and coaching of all students in their curriculum. The result of successful strategic instruction helps fulfill the global Standard 10 of the CCSS—students should *Read and comprehend complex literary and informational texts independently and proficiently.*

Thanks to Jennifer Berne and Sophie Degener for providing this clear and complete guide for middle grade teachers and students.

Donna Ogle

Acknowledgments

It has been our great privilege to work with middle school teachers throughout the Chicago area who have helped us to see the importance of continuing small group strategic reading instruction into the middle grades, and have provided us input in figuring out how best to do that, particularly given the unique circumstances of middle school teachers and students. We appreciate these teachers' openness to new ideas and willingness to give strategic reading groups a try, most often with great success.

We are also exceedingly grateful to our colleagues at Neah-Kah-Nie Middle School in Rockaway Beach, Oregon, who have taught us so much about what it takes to scaffold teachers into this practice. Thanks, particularly, to Jim Severson, a remarkable middle school principal who believes that all leaders are learners and has pushed our thinking about the ways that administrators can best support innovative middle school literacy practices.

We have also been fortunate to have an amazing group of National Louis University doctoral students who, through a research internship, tried out our model for strategic reading groups with students at their schools and then provided professional development on strategic reading groups to the teachers at their schools. Throughout this work, they provided us with specific feedback that has helped us fine-tune our own professional development work with teachers and school districts, which in turn has directly impacted the writing of this book. For support for these doctoral interns, we thank the International Reading Association who awarded us a Gertrude Whipple Professional Development grant that funded a portion of their work. Special thanks go to Shirley Davidson, a doctoral student who not only worked with students and teachers on strategic reading groups but also reviewed the research on middle school literacy and small group instruction in the middle grades.

We are thrilled to be working with Corwin, and in particular, we would like to thank Carol Collins, who has supported our work on this book, provided helpful ideas for making the book better, and demonstrated a sound understanding of why this work is so important. We are also grateful to the reviewers of this book, who brought a keen understanding of middle school dynamics and needs that helped shape our revisions in ways that will make the ideas contained herein even more meaningful to middle school teachers.

Finally, as always, we have learned so much from our own children, Allyson, Justin, Luke, and Peter. We send them off to school each day, hopeful that their teachers will listen carefully to what they can do and support them in what they can almost do. We wrote this book with the belief that our own children's teachers might read it. For us, there is no more important audience.

Publisher's Acknowledgments

Corwin gratefully acknowledges the contributions of the following reviewers:

David Callaway, Language Arts Teacher
Rocky Heights Middle School
Parker, CO

Julia Dewees, English and Social Science Teacher
Vista del Mar Middle School
CUSD BTSA/Induction Program Staff Teacher Development System
San Clemente, CA

Rachel Hanson, Gifted Eighth-Grade Language Arts
Lakeside Middle School
Cumming, GA

Patricia (Patti) Hendricks, Seventh-Grade Language Arts Teacher
Sunset Ridge Middle School
West Jordan, UT

Melanie Mares, Language Arts Teacher Leader
Lowndes Middle School
Valdosta, GA

Rachel B. McMillan, Literacy Coach
Ocean Lakes HS / Corporate Landing MS
Virginia Beach, VA

Lyndon Oswald, Principal
Sandcreek Middle School
Ammon, ID

Ann Richardson, Coordinator of Gifted/Language Arts—Secondary
Fayette County Schools
Fayette County, GA

Joseph Staub, Teacher (Resource Specialist)
Thomas Starr King Middle School
Los Angeles, CA

Michelle Strom, Language Arts Teacher
Carson Middle School
Colorado Springs, CO

About the Authors

Jennifer Berne, PhD, is an Associate Professor and Department Chair of Reading and Language at National Louis University. She teaches courses in the teaching of writing and the teaching of comprehension. She is also an active staff developer, working in K–12 classrooms in implementing best practices in contemporary reading and writing.

Sophie C. Degener, EdD, is an Assistant Professor in the Reading and Language Department at National Louis University, where she teaches literacy methods to preservice teachers as well as courses in beginning reading and reading research. She works with many school districts around the Chicago area on the topics of balanced literacy and differentiated instruction.

1

Introduction

This book introduces instruction in strategic, differentiated reading groups for middle school classrooms. Small group reading instruction has a long history in elementary and middle schools. Until fifteen years ago, small group instruction was most often a place where students sat with their teachers to work on reading skills. These groups allowed the teacher to give different instruction to different groups of students as the teacher saw fit. Most teachers remember, from their own experience as students or from teaching long ago, that these groups were stable in their membership. Students were placed in groups in September and they stayed in those same groups for the year. More recently, *guided reading* groups (Fountas & Pinnell, 1996; Opitz & Ford, 2001) have focused upon reading strategies and are, notably, flexible in membership, with students moving in and out as their literacy skills and strategies develop at different rates. The field owes a tremendous debt to the scholars who helped us see the value of flexibility in these groups for all grades and reading levels.

Strategic, differentiated reading groups come out of our work in K–5 reading instruction. In working with K–5 teachers on guided reading we discovered that despite their best intentions, they were often unable to do guided reading as often or as well as they would have liked. Part of the struggle, our further inquiry suggested, was that the groups went on too long to be productive for the rest of the students. Part of the struggle was that planning lessons for multiple groups was unrealistic given a teacher's other responsibilities and limited time; another part of the struggle had to do with the difficulty in implementing effective practices inside the group. We offered elementary teachers a simpler model for guided reading that we call *responsive guided reading groups* (see Berne & Degener, 2010, for more

1

detail on the way these groups function in elementary classrooms). As we began working in K–8 buildings (which are the norm in the large urban area in which we work), the middle school teachers asked about adapting these groups for the needs of adolescent readers. We had always believed these groups would be effective with readers of all ages, though middle school teachers often shy away from small group instruction. Some avoid small group instruction because they believe the groups feel so elementary. Some avoid it because they have no experience seeing it with students in these grades. Still others avoid it because the groups can be cumbersome, time intensive, and inelegant. We see the promise of these groups, and also the difficulty, and offer middle school teachers a model that, we believe, maximizes the value while minimizing the struggles.

Before we present a detailed discussion of the small group work we recommend for middle school teachers and students, we discuss the ways that middle school language arts teachers differentiate throughout their literacy block. It is important that differentiation not be relegated only to small group instruction, but a vital component of everything we do with students. We feel it important to embed our discussion of small group instruction in our bigger ideas about the entire literacy block. Thus, we begin with an overview discussion of the conceptual ideas underpinning excellence in middle school literacy instruction. Chapter 2 presents a more detailed discussion of where and when various instructional practices fit into a middle school day.

DIFFERENTIATED LITERATURE INSTRUCTION

Middle school language arts teachers are most often asked to teach two subjects at once. They are, of course, responsible for the demands of literature as a content area. In this course of study, they teach students about the characteristics of various literary genres; story and fictional text structure; figurative language; literary periods and authors; and archetypal plots, themes, and character traits. Middle school teachers are often anxious to share the stories, poetry, and drama that they loved when they were students with the students they find in front of them. Our observations of dozens of middle school language arts teachers suggests that in large measure, teachers are comfortable and skilled at selecting and sharing rich classic and contemporary young adult literature.

In the last dozen or so years, there has been much attention focused upon the ways in which teachers deliver this content. Book clubs, literature circles, and other small group interactions have helped teachers involve more students in their own learning. These structures have also allowed opportunities for teachers to provide different texts for different level students. We are always thrilled to see students discussing literature on their own and almost never fail to get excited along with them as they talk together about wonderful books, poems, and other kinds of texts.

There are times, however, when a teacher determines that the entire class will read the same novel. In this case, differentiation of support is essential. The following example highlights the work of an exemplary sixth-grade teacher as she organizes her literature instruction to differentiate for student levels:

> Ms. Simon's sixth-grade students are reading Lois Lowry's dystopian novel *The Giver*. As in many middle school classes, Ms. Simon's students have a wide range of reading abilities. Some students read at a second- or third-grade level, while others have no problem with high school–level reading. Even so, Ms. Simon has determined that all students should have access to this novel, which is rich in thematic importance and always evokes strong opinions and lively discussion from students. When assigning reading to be done independently in class or as homework, Ms. Simon knows that her strongest readers will need little support and will easily comprehend the basic story. She knows the thematic complexity will come out in class discussion and in their writing, so she leaves them alone on their initial read. Her largest population of students, those reading right around grade level, will be able to make meaning of the plot with some support. For this group, she designs a readers' guide that previews vocabulary, offers chapter summaries before each chapter, and suggests guiding questions. She instructs this group to use this guide to assist their reading and to ask for more support if necessary. For her lowest level readers, she provides an audio version, downloaded from a school supported online source, in which the author herself reads the slightly abridged text. The students read along on their versions, and Ms. Simon alerts them to the fact that some passages may be shortened or skipped. These students will be able to participate in class discussion of the text as the themes, plot, and figurative language are available to them through their listening skills.

This is an example of differentiated literature instruction. Clearly, the priority is access to the ideas in the text and this is accomplished for different students in different ways. If all students can comprehend, talk, and write about *The Giver*, Ms. Simon's instruction has been successful. We greatly admire this classroom example because even though the three groups of students access the text in different ways, their varied reading levels do not keep them from sharing the experience of an age-appropriate text. A decade earlier, all the students might have received the same instruction on this text. It would have been simple for some, a challenge for others, and nearly impossible for those who struggled, and we didn't do much about that. Though we have learned much about differentiation in the past decades, these practices persist in some classrooms today. Ms. Simon is able to differentiate, allowing students to learn different things in different ways, but still to share the experience of a text she believes is worthy of study. Certainly, there are times when Ms. Simon has groups reading different novels, but not all times. Struggling readers deserve access to texts at their social level, even if they cannot read them independently. They are most often given texts that are below grade level—which makes sense—but these texts are also frequently below their social level. Simple, elementary texts are demotivating for middle school readers who may be quite mature in their thinking and understanding even if their reading level is low. We want to expose all middle school students to texts that are at their social level even if the texts are well above their reading level. The preceding example depicts this possibility.

Strategic Reading Instruction

In addition to this kind of literature discussion, and often in the same class period, middle school teachers are responsible for teaching what we call *strategic reading*. Strategic reading instruction calls for different teaching practices, different kinds of texts, and different assessments than does literature instruction. This does not mean that students don't read literature strategically, only that strategic reading instruction has different primary aims and purposes than does literature instruction.

With strategic reading instruction, the focus is not on the text at hand but on the way that one *reads a text*. Strategic reading instruction aims for students to gain experience using reading strategies that transfer across time and texts. Because of this, understanding the content of the text is less important than the lessons learned about reading.

Compare the following example of strategic reading instruction with the example of literature instruction found earlier:

> The eighth graders in Ms. Thomas's class watch and listen as she cognitively models her own reading of an article from the *New York Times*, "Orchestras on Big Screens: Chase Scenes Needed?" (2010) about the new movement in the arts, wherein technicians beam orchestral concerts to theaters around the country so that these performances might be watched in real time. She reads and thinks aloud to model for her students her own reading process. The actual text appears in bold; her thinking aloud is in italics:
>
> > **The performing arts have long been holdouts for unfiltered, direct connection between audiences and performers in a digitized, electronic and screen-laden world** (p. A1). *Okay, I am thinking that they are saying that fancy things like opera and symphony usually are snobby about television but now maybe they are changing their mind. I think that is what they are saying, but I am going to read it again just to be*

sure. [reads aloud] *Okay, yep, that is what they are saying. I am going to go on.*

Opera houses, ballet companies, even the National Theater in London, are competing to lure audiences to live high-definition broadcasts in movie theaters, many of which are then shown again. It is the HD-ification of the arts, and it is already affecting programming decisions along with costume and set design, lighting choices and even ticket prices (p. A1). *Hmm, there is definitely a word I do not know in all that and it seems like an important one. HD-ification. So I think I am going to look at the word and see if I can understand any of the parts. I know that HD usually stands for high definition because I have an HD television at home, and I think "ification" means something like doing something like certification means to certify, so from that I am going to make an inference that HD-ification means becoming high definition. That seems to work in that sentence so I am going to go with it.*

Ms. Thomas then asks her students to summarize what they saw her do. One student points out that she reread a part that she wasn't sure of and another student noted that she used things she knows about words to infer the meaning of an unknown word. Ms. Thomas repeats these strategies, copies them on chart paper, and tells students that they will now practice using the same strategies they watched her use. Ms. Thomas pulls three small stacks of texts out of her file cabinet. For her highest readers, she distributes an article on the president's recent visit to China. For her middle readers, she hands out a piece of a long article on organic farming. For those who struggle, she offers a section of their social studies textbook on immigration. Each student begins to read their text as Ms. Thomas reminds them of the two strategies they witnessed her using and she hopes they will focus upon as they read texts that she assures them are "quite a challenge."

Ms. Thomas knows that students need to learn how to read strategically on texts that are in their zone of proximal development (Vygotsky, 1978) or just beyond what they can do on their own. She also knows that there are varied levels in her class. If she were to distribute the same text to all students, some would read it with ease, for others it would be a modest struggle, and still others would be frustrated no matter how much support was offered. Her wise solution is to teach a common lesson to all and then ask students to practice the modeled strategy on a text that is at an appropriate level for their learning. Ms. Thomas worries little about the content of the text; instead, her focus in text selection is on finding something that will be a modest challenge for each group. Ms. Thomas thought it was very reasonable to categorize student readers in three groups for this purpose, though some teachers might divide the class into more than three groups. She did not pick the texts in order for students to learn content or share an experience of reading, so she picked three different topics that coincided with the reading level for which she was looking. In this, she was able to modestly challenge each group. Ms. Thomas is well aware that students will note that there are different levels of reading. She makes great efforts to group students in all sorts of ways, for all sorts of purposes, throughout her language arts instruction so that all levels of students interact around books and writing. For this activity, however, she lets the students know that she has selected texts that she believes are appropriate for their learning.

THE NEED FOR BOTH LITERATURE AND STRATEGIC READING INSTRUCTION

The examples of Ms. Simon and Ms. Thomas exemplify two crucial, yet distinct, teaching practices and are summarized in Table 1.1. The first shows differentiation in the teaching of the same literary text. All students in Ms. Simon's class read the same text, yet the support for their reading was different. The second shows instruction in strategic reading with multiple texts, customized to student level. In this example, students in Ms. Thomas's class received the same lesson, but practiced the strategy on different texts. In Chapter 2, we discuss in detail the placement of both of these kinds of instruction in a middle school language arts classroom or literacy block. These two emphases (along with an emphasis on writing and self-selected pleasure reading) will provide students with the necessary tools for accelerating their skill in reading all kinds of texts.

Table 1.1   Literature Instruction and Strategic Reading Instruction

	Texts	*Genre*	*Support*	*Emphasis*
Literature instruction	Same for all	Novel Poetry Drama Creative nonfiction	Varied	Text content Theme Character Plot Figurative language Literature enjoyment
Strategic reading instruction	Differentiated by instructional level	Nonfiction/ informational texts Content-area textbooks	Same for all	Reading strategies

STRATEGIC READING GROUPS

The work that Ms. Thomas did with her whole class is critical in introducing them to new strategies for managing difficult texts. In addition to this instruction, students need to work in close proximity to their teachers, in small groups. The small group instruction we will describe provides the opportunity for teachers to listen to students read aloud individually—a rare and extremely valuable opportunity for middle grade teachers. When students read aloud, teachers can hear their strengths and can identify areas of concern. They also can provide ad hoc strategy instruction that arises directly from a student miscue or comprehension breakdown. There is compelling research (e.g., Durkin, 1993; Wilkinson & Anderson, 1995) to suggest that students gain little from round-robin reading (i.e., reading aloud while other students follow along), but they do need to read aloud to skilled adults who can use what they hear as a valuable formative assessment. Strategic, differentiated reading groups focus on individual student reading, which results in a customized teacher cue that the student can take away from the group and practice independently. Chapters 4 and 5 focus upon helping middle grade teachers learn how to listen to readers and provide appropriate cues.

Teachers want to do the kind of intense, effective instruction that small group instruction allows. They believe that students benefit from one-on-one attention focused upon their individual reading; however, the organization and management involved in setting up and enacting the groups completely overwhelms them. In response to this, we have put together a simplified model of small group strategic reading instruction that is manageable for new teachers and teachers new to small group instruction of this kind. In particular, we have listened carefully to teachers' concerns about text selection, planning, time management, and engaging the other students in productive independent work. We begin this discussion with the principles we relied upon to create the model. Then we offer an outline of the activities and timing to use as a template for getting started. Each of these principles is elaborated upon and instantiated in classroom practices in the chapters that follow. For now, we offer a practical and conceptual overview.

Strategic reading groups have a predictable, transparent structure.

Adolescents and teachers benefit from routine, particularly when they engage in the kind of challenging work that takes place in strategic, differentiated reading groups. For this reason, these groups run the same way each time. Later in this chapter, we provide a very specific "schedule" complete with timing, yet we offer this only as a model. We hope that teachers think about the spirit in which all the elements are included and make decisions about how their time should be allotted in these groups.

In strategic reading groups, the teacher waits for the student to miscue or have a comprehension breakdown before deciding what to teach. Thus, the preplanning is limited.

In a strategic reading group, student errors dictate instruction. It is the student's reading that tells the teacher what the student might learn in that moment. Consider the following example:

> Ari is a seventh-grader working with his teacher, Mr. Sanchez, in a strategic reading group. He reads a passage from an April 30, 2010, *New York Times* article on the Gulf oil spill that his teacher believed would be a challenge for him and his like-leveled classmates.

Ari:	Officials in the Obama administration began for the first time Friday to publicly chast . . . chast . . . chasten?
Mr. Sanchez:	Okay, I hear you are struggling with that word so I am going to stop you there. Why not go back and read the same sentence again, seeing if thinking about the beginning of the sentence might help you with that word.
Ari:	Officials in the Obama administration began for the first time Friday to publicly . . . [stops reading]
Mr. Sanchez:	Okay, that didn't seem to solve it. I think we might want to try to guess at the meaning of the word, which I will tell you is pronounced "chastise"—is that a word you know?
Ari:	No.
Mr. Sanchez:	Okay, well, one thing I do when I come to a word I don't know is I see if I can guess at it by thinking about the meaning of the sentence. What is it that we know about the sentence before that word? What is it about?
Ari:	About the president doing something for the first time.
Mr. Sanchez:	Good, but that probably doesn't give us enough to go on, so let's skip that word and keep reading and see if the end of this part helps us to better understand that word and that sentence.
Ari:	BP America for its handling of the spreading oil gusher in the Gulf of Mexico, calling the oil company's current

resources. . . . Oh, I think they might mean yells at or something.

Mr. Sanchez: That is right, Ari. That is great. Look what you did: You used the rest of the sentence to figure out a word you didn't know. I want you to continue to read and when that happens again, remember what we did. Sometimes later in the sentence there is a clue to a word you don't know. I am really impressed with how you did that.

The next student may very well read a different page and Mr. Sanchez will likely cue that student on a different word in a different way. He also might cue the next student on a comprehension learning strategy rather than a vocabulary learning strategy. Mr. Sanchez's goal is not to teach about any one word or any one text in particular, but rather to build the students' repertoire of strategies to use when they come to any unknown word or encounter any misunderstanding as they read during their school and afterschool day.

The materials chosen for strategic reading groups need not be thematically connected or integrated into the rest of the curriculum.

One of the largest drains on teacher time and energy is attempting to thematically link strategic reading texts across performance levels. If teachers believe that they have to come up with five texts, at different levels, all on the same topic, they might find themselves spending all their time in the book room pulling texts or on the computer locating online reading materials. In strategic reading groups, the goal is learning how to read beyond the text at hand, so the text becomes a tool for learning a new strategy. In this respect, the actual content is not as crucial as the strategies learned. There are many times in the literacy day when content is very, very important, when we try to use reading to engage students with literature or other content-area curriculum. We would never say that content is not important in teaching a student to read better, but rather that in a context like strategic reading groups, we aren't nearly as worried about it.

It behooves us to be honest with students and let them know that in school there are lots of times to read really wonderful books; they hear them as we read them aloud; they select them to read to themselves during independent reading. We also sometimes use books to learn particular things. In the strategic reading group, the texts we use may not always be entirely engaging. That isn't why we picked these books. Just like football players spend time in the tedium of weight lifting and doing running drills during practice so their skills might be sharper during the game, we sometimes use books lacking in rich literary merit to help students learn and practice strategies that will help them in other, richer, reading experiences.

Strategic reading groups are designed to force students to miscue or have a comprehension breakdown while they have a supportive person with them, thus the texts must be difficult enough to force an error in a short amount of time.

Most teachers are familiar with the notion of independent-, instructional-, and frustration-level texts. An independent-level book is one that a student can read easily and comfortably such that explicit instruction in strategy use is not required for good comprehension. A book is at a student's instructional level if the student can make meaning of it with some support. This is the place where literacy educators (e.g., Dorn, French, & Jones, 1998; Fountas & Pinnell, 1996) believe students have the most opportunity to learn. Because the text challenges are just beyond their grasp, a teacher's or other skillful reader's support may be enough to help the student make meaning. The hope is that this immediate instruction will be transferable so that when the student encounters a similar text challenge when reading independently, the student will employ the strategy, and thus propel to new reading capabilities. A frustration-level text is one far beyond a student's ability and will likely agitate that student, even with teacher support. Teachers should refrain from asking students to learn from something that is clearly beyond their current abilities.

In strategic reading groups, teachers should plan to use texts that they believe will cause students to miscue or display a strategy breakdown fairly quickly, within a minute for middle school readers. If a student goes on too long without struggle, teachers lose the opportunity to assist, as they need to get on to the next student.

Many teachers remind students that the purpose of the strategic reading group is to force errors; they tell them not to be ashamed or worried if they struggle because the book was chosen so that they will. Though this is an odd concept for students and teachers, repetition of such a reminder will surely smooth out some of the discomfort.

It is counterintuitive to wish students to struggle at a task. So much of a teacher's job is to help students succeed. However, in a strategic reading group, teachers are able to customize their instruction because students demonstrate ineffective strategy use as they read. Without this breakdown, the teacher is left only to encourage students to keep reading. When a teacher notes that a student has no difficulties with a text that the other group members do struggle with, it is worth considering moving the student to another group. Similarly, if a student struggles more than the other group members, it may indicate that the text is at the student's frustration level, and not an appropriate text level for reasonable instruction in any context.

Strategic reading groups should be brief (12–15 minutes per group).

One of the most dramatic differences between strategic reading groups and other kinds of small group reading instruction is that they are purposefully brief. We designed them for teachers just getting their feet wet in this kind of instruction. Most teachers, even those brand new to the field, can help the rest of the class work quietly on independent, group, or paired literacy work for short amounts of time. Engaging other students in meaningful work while the teacher works with a small group is crucial, yet it is unrealistic to believe that this might be done for more than short amounts of time. Generally, teachers who use the model we describe see two groups per day. Thus, the remaining students are asked to behave and work well together or independently (or both, depending on the preference of the teacher, the grade, and the context) for up to 15 minutes in two different sessions—first as the teacher works with the first group and then after a 5 minute break and possible redirection of the remainder of the class, as the teacher works with the second group. The subsequent section details the timing of the actual activities as they are done in the strategic reading groups.

Teaching that can be effectively done with the whole class is not the focus of strategic reading groups; rather, instruction is limited to that which can only be done in this context.

Any lesson that can be done as a whole group lesson is not typically part of strategic reading groups. The value of placing students in these groups is that the teacher has the ability to listen to students read alone, an activity that cannot be done with the whole group. Because this is such a crucial endeavor in helping kids to read better, any activities that take away from that time should be moved into the large group context or another teaching mode. For example, Ms. Lowe sees that her most capable reading group could benefit from asking questions about the text as they read to themselves, in order to improve their comprehension. However, to teach this strategy well, she would need to explain and model using the questioning strategy, something that would take up the entire time (or more) allotted for this group. Far more effective would be to teach and model questioning during a lesson with her whole class—a lesson like the one described earlier when Ms. Thomas thought aloud and then set up opportunities for guided practice, so her students might do the same. In that way, each of her students, regardless of their reading capabilities, would be exposed to an important comprehension strategy, and each of them would see how a competent reader uses that strategy. After modeling questioning with the whole group and having students practice asking questions using texts at their instructional level, Ms. Lowe could refer to this strategy while working with a student in a strategic reading group.

If she hears Latasha reading in a monotone fashion, indicating that she might not be appropriately monitoring her understanding, she might say,

> While I was reading the article on nuclear fusion to the whole class yesterday, remember that you saw me question myself as I read. When you ask questions while you read, it helps you to better understand what you know and what you still need to find out. I would like you to try to read that passage again, stopping to ask a question while I listen. Let's see if that helps you to better understand this difficult passage.

In this way, Ms. Lowe asks Latasha to begin using, individually, a strategy she was exposed to during whole group instruction.

THE STRUCTURE OF A STRATEGIC READING GROUP

As illustrated with the concepts discussed previously, it is very important for strategic reading groups to be structured tightly and consistently. A model (with approximate timing) follows, one that we have found to be successful with middle school teachers and students. Each element will be discussed in detail in chapters to follow.

1. Teacher reminds students of the purpose of the group and of the necessity for the text to be a challenge (less than 30 seconds).

2. Teacher refers students to a previously discussed strategy that may be relevant in this text for many of the students (less than 30 seconds).

3. Teacher directs students to continue to read silently (30 seconds).

4. Teacher circulates to each student, listening to them read until they miscue or otherwise demonstrate a comprehension breakdown. Teacher coaches student through a strategy designed to help with the error.

5. Teacher moves to each student and repeats Step 4 (2 minutes per student, with 5 students = 10 minutes).

6. Teacher asks students to stop reading and close their books (30 seconds).

7. Teacher summarizes the strategy worked on with each student and asks students to pay close attention to using the strategy for the rest of the day, in reading, as they study other subjects, and at home (2 minutes).

8. Teacher calls the next groups and repeats Steps 1 through 7.

This whole process takes less than 15 minutes. With groups of four, it is even quicker.

OVERVIEW OF REMAINDER OF BOOK

We are anxious for middle school teachers to try this kind of instruction because we see how effective it is, how much students benefit, and how comfortable teachers feel doing it once they have had time to study it and practice. We have set up the rest of the book to support teachers in understanding how the structure works, how to cue students during strategic grouping, how to find materials, how to assess and group students, and how to manage the rest of the class. We have organized the text to concentrate on the detailed work inside the group before sharing chapters on some of the bigger picture—assessment, selecting materials, and managing the rest of the class. Readers who might prefer to understand the role of those important components prior to really digging into the work of the groups might wish to read the chapters in a slightly different order. To accommodate these different preferences, we next briefly summarize the chapters in the order that they appear in the book. Following the summary, an alternative order is suggested.

Chapter 1: Introduction to strategic reading groups. This chapter presents a strategic and conceptual overview of how and why these groups function in a middle school literacy classroom.

Chapter 2: Fitting strategic reading groups into the middle school literacy block. This chapter briefly outlines the essential components of balanced literacy and suggests time frames that correspond to different configurations (i.e., the same period for reading and language arts, block schedules, reading and language arts taught separately, short periods, longer periods) that may be found in middle schools or junior highs. In particular, we offer ideas for fitting strategic reading groups into reading instruction no matter how the literacy day is organized.

Chapter 3: A detailed look at strategic reading groups. This chapter introduces readers to the particulars of how the groups function including activities, suggested timing, size of groups, and student and teacher roles.

Chapter 4: Listening to fluent readers. This first "how-to" chapter discusses the difficult and exciting task of listening to middle grade student readers in order to recognize each of their strengths and weaknesses as a reader.

Chapter 5: Teacher cueing during informational text reading. Once teachers understand how to listen to student reading, and what it is they are hearing as they listen, they need to see how they can intervene when student reading reveals a suspected breakdown in meaning making. This chapter helps teachers to recognize what cues help students when they are struggling to understand informational texts like those they encounter in their content-area coursework.

Chapter 6: Teacher cueing during narrative text reading. When teachers work with students on reading of narratives, they employ a slightly different set of cues. This chapter introduces cueing for the reading of narratives like those they most often encounter in their English classes.

Chapter 7: Materials for strategic reading groups. Though the preceding three chapters argue that the most important "material" is teacher knowledge, there is certainly a need for texts to use in these groups. This chapter offers teachers ideas for the kinds of texts most effective for the kind of teaching promoted in these groups, especially focusing upon what they already have in their rooms and buildings or can acquire free of charge.

Chapter 8: Assessment prior to and during strategic reading groups. Students are assessed at the beginning of the year in order to initially compose the groups. Unlike reading groups of old, however, ongoing assessment allows flexibility in group membership. This chapter helps teachers with simple ways to group at the beginning of the year and with ways to keep track of student progress as the year goes along.

Chapter 9: Managing the rest of the class during strategic guided reading groups. We continually reinforce to teachers that nobody is ready to start working in these groups until everyone who is not in the groups can self-manage as they engage in independent literacy activities. This chapter discusses the management of the rest of the students so that the teacher is free to work hard with the students in the group.

Alternative Order

For those teachers who prefer to know how to group, select materials, and manage the rest of the students prior to learning about the intricacies of the group instruction, we recommend reading this text in the following order:

Chapter 1: Introduction

Chapter 2: Fitting strategic reading groups into the middle school literacy block

Chapter 9: Managing the rest of the class during strategic reading groups

Chapter 8: Assessment prior to and during strategic reading groups

Chapter 7: Materials for strategic reading groups

Chapter 3: A detailed look at strategic reading groups

Chapter 4: Listening to fluent readers

Chapter 5: Teacher cueing for informational texts

Chapter 6: Teacher cueing for narrative texts

One Final Note

This text has an ample number of charts and figures that some teachers may want to reproduce for themselves or their students. These can be accessed in reproducible form on our publisher sponsored website at www.corwin.com/strategicreadinggroups.

2

Fitting Strategic Reading Groups Into the Middle School Literacy Block

Excellent middle school teachers balance skill and strategy instruction with the use of quality literature and reading and writing for authentic purposes. You can't have one without the other. We believe strongly that teachers should not begin strategic reading groups unless independent reading and literature enjoyment are already prioritized in their classrooms. Students need to see that the kind of reading they will do in strategic reading groups allows them to become better readers, and that their improvement will expand the universe of really great books they can read independently.

In support of the balance just described, teachers use a combination of grouping strategies—whole class, small group, pairs, and individual—in order to best meet the instructional needs of all students in class.

Balanced literacy instruction is accepted as best practice for both elementary and middle schools, yet middle school teachers often struggle to provide this balance, given the constraints of a departmentalized schedule and curriculum. In particular, they seem to struggle with grouping students and differentiating materials. Research suggests that in middle schools, teachers tend to rely too heavily on traditional lecture formats, with round-robin reading of grade-level texts and few if any small group opportunities for students to engage with texts at their own instructional levels (Blanton, Wood, & Taylor, 2010).

Small group differentiated reading instruction is often perceived as something that only elementary school teachers do, but in truth, we know that many adolescent readers still struggle with reading and would benefit from differentiated instruction in middle school. Additionally, we know that even the strongest readers deserve to be challenged by increasingly difficult texts, something that will not happen if they are always working with grade-level materials.

INSTRUCTIONAL PRACTICES IN BALANCED MIDDLE SCHOOL LITERACY INSTRUCTION

The following is a list of practices that belong in middle school literacy instruction:

- Shared reading
- Strategic reading groups
- Independent reading
- Teacher read aloud
- Writing
- Literature study, including whole class novel study and literature circles
- Word study, including spelling and vocabulary instruction

Note that these practices are not exclusive to middle school language arts teachers. Many of these practices can and should be reinforced in the content areas. For example, science teachers may bring in trade books on topics currently being studied, so that students have the opportunity to read independently and expand their knowledge of science content. Social studies teachers may choose to read a historical novel aloud in order to build background knowledge about a new unit of study. Math teachers certainly teach vocabulary to help students better understand new concepts. We encourage teachers across the content areas to consider how they can reinforce literacy practices in their own classes.

There are many fine books that detail these practices; our purpose here is not to describe them in detail, but rather to show where strategic reading groups fit in among these practices. Table 2.1 looks at materials, grouping, teacher support provided, and the instructional emphasis of each literacy practice.

Table 2.1 Important Literacy Practices in Middle School Language Arts

Literacy Practice	Materials	Grouping	Teacher Support	Instructional Emphasis
Shared reading (strategic reading)	Teacher selected, high quality	Whole group (with small group guided practice)	High—teacher-led lessons followed by teacher-supported practice	Comprehension and vocabulary strategies
Strategic reading groups	**Teacher selected, quality not the focus**	**Small homogeneous groups**	**High—student reading emphasized, but with teacher providing needed, and sometimes intensive, support**	**Reinforcement of strategies taught during shared reading**
Independent reading	Student-selected, high interest	Individual	Low—just as a guide in text selection	Reading practice Engagement, enjoyment
Teacher read aloud	Teacher-selected, high quality	Whole group	Medium low—occasional clarification of meaning or vocabulary word	Engagement, enjoyment Exposure to rich texts and vocabulary
Writing	Student-selected topics	Varies: different at different stages of the writing process	Varies (high, medium, and low)	Writing process: drafting, revising, editing, publishing Multiple genres
Literature study	Teacher-selected, high quality; students choose from teacher-selected books for literature circles	Whole class (novel study); small group (literature circles)	High during whole class work; medium or low during literature circles	Text content Theme Character Plot Figurative language Enjoyment
Word study	Teacher-selected, based on student needs	Small homogeneous groups	Depends on needs and abilities of groups	Word recognition Knowledge of word parts Spelling strategies

Table 2.1 demonstrates how these practices are distinct and bring balance to the language arts block. Notice that teachers usually choose materials, but that there are also times when students can choose their own materials, as in independent reading, writing, and literature circles. Grouping practices range from whole class, to small group, to individual, and within some literacy practices (like writing), there can be multiple grouping practices for different purposes. Teacher support also varies, and some practices require more support than others. Note that instructional emphases also vary widely, with engagement and enjoyment emphasized in independent reading and teacher read aloud, while strategy work is emphasized in other areas.

A DETAILED LOOK AT MATERIALS USED THROUGHOUT THE LITERACY BLOCK

This book's emphasis is on strategic reading groups, and in examination of Table 2.1, we see that teachers select texts for use in these groups with little consideration for literary merit. This can be upsetting to many teachers who believe we should use high-quality texts no matter what. However, when we look across Table 2.1, we see that as long as teachers nest their strategic reading groups within the other practices, they will expose students to great texts multiple times each day, during independent reading, teacher read aloud, and shared reading.

The kinds of materials that a teacher selects for strategic reading instruction will be different than those selected for literature study. In literature study, teachers select texts that have particular literary value and are ideal for teaching children about genre, or for doing an author study, or for looking at a particular literary element. Teachers may also decide to have children read books, or they may read books aloud, that have great thematic richness. To enhance these reading experiences, teachers may arrange book club groups or literature circle discussions so children can deepen their thinking about these books.

In addition to this instruction in literature, as part of the literacy classroom, teachers arrange for students to select their own books—which may be fiction or nonfiction. These are the kinds of books that students read easily and select because they are of interest.

Clearly, there are a lot of texts present in a balanced literacy classroom, and each can take on different, important roles. We hope that teachers will understand the difference between materials used for strategic reading groups and those used for other purposes. Strategic reading books are those that will be outside of students' comfortable reading, so they will not be the same as those that students select themselves for independent reading or that teachers select for a read aloud or classroom novel study.

Strategic reading materials also will not include great works of literature, which require lots of thematic support and invite great discussion, activities that are not done much, if at all, during strategic reading instruction.

We try to discourage teachers from picking great books for strategic reading groups, as these groups are a place to practice reading, not to read for engagement. Students read only a little at a time, and they often do so with great difficulty—by design. Using great literature in these groups would be a waste of much of the beauty and importance of great literature. Consider the following example from a strategic reading group in Mr. Austen's sixth-grade classroom. Here he listens to Jason read aloud from Gary Paulsen's (2000) novel *Hatchet*:

Jason: The pilot was having a heart attack and even as the knowledge came to Brian he saw the pilot slam into the seat one more time, one more awful time he slammed back into the seat and his right leg jerked, pulling the plane to the side in a sudden twist and his head fell forward and spit came. (p. 11)

Mr. Austen: Okay, so what do you think is happening in this passage?

Jason: Brian is watching this guy fly the plane?

Mr. Austen: You don't sound sure. What can you do to check if your idea is correct?

Jason: Well, I could go back and reread.

Mr. Austen: That's a great strategy. Why don't you try that and then let me know if you have a better idea of what's happening in this passage.

Mr. Austen executed this interaction just fine. The trouble is that *Hatchet* is the kind of book that commands attention to the larger themes and ideas. The section Jason and Mr. Austen were reading together is genuinely engaging and students deserve to listen to or read it in an uninterrupted fashion, during teacher read aloud or independent reading. Using it during a strategic reading group takes away from the power of the novel and certainly contributes to students' frustration, as they are never allowed to delve in deeper to this novel as a whole.

We like to encourage teachers to save some kinds of reading experiences, like the read aloud of a fantastic book like *Hatchet,* just for the pure experience of reading. We often want to allow students the opportunity to forget their surroundings and sink into the text, to enter an author-created world. These kinds of experiences are shown to have tremendous benefits for students' listening comprehension, vocabulary development, and feelings about reading. In turn, listening comprehension, vocabulary development, and feelings about reading all have been shown to benefit student reading achievement. This is an important point. Reading to kids and allowing kids to read to themselves for the simple experience of doing so makes them more fluent and able to read increasingly difficult texts (e.g., Cullinan, 2000; Samuels, 2006), just as the explicit teaching of strategies we do in small group strategic reading instruction also contributes to their growing competency. This is part of the balance we discuss in the term *balanced literacy.* There are indeed times to work hard on texts with the necessary support, and often interruption, of a teacher. There are other times when no such interruption is necessary or desirable.

We absolutely believe that strategic reading groups fit into a balanced literacy classroom, yet we would never use them as the exclusive route to increasing student reading ability. Without exposure to great books that students can read independently, and without exposure to fine literature, the use of strategies is almost for naught. We know that the best preparation for any future reading task is to create conditions whereby students become readers for life. Lifetime readers are lifetime readers because they choose to be, often because of their exposure to amazing books. It would be very difficult to find a middle school student who was "turned into a reader" via instruction in strategic reading groups.

The distinction between practicing reading and reading is a fine one. We practice reading in strategic reading groups. This practice isn't always fun or interesting (much like training for a sport isn't always as much fun as playing the sport), but it is necessary to get better and experience the joy of reading. First, though, we want to make sure that students are given opportunities to read independently, for enjoyment.

Once teachers are certain that students are engaging with books that they have chosen, and reading them independently without challenges, teachers should begin instruction in reading with books that may cause students a bit of disequilibrium. We believe that students must be modestly challenged in order to invoke, intentionally, new and familiar strategies so that they continue to push themselves as readers. Recall from Chapter 1 that students will struggle when they come to strategic reading groups, and the groups are set up for just that purpose.

Fitting It All Together

It can be challenging enough to consider all the pieces that must be in place within the middle-level literacy block: what they entail, what materials are needed, and how they are distinguished from each other. Harder still is considering how to put all the pieces together into a manageable schedule. Tables 2.2, 2.3, and 2.4 consider three typical schedules for

Table 2.2 Middle School Literacy Instruction, Block Schedule (80 minutes per day)

Monday	Tuesday	Wednesday	Thursday	Friday
• Read aloud (15 minutes) • Shared reading (15 minutes) • Strategic reading groups, including independent reading and writing (35 minutes) • Word study (15 minutes)	• Read aloud (10 minutes) • Writing (40 minutes) • Literature study, including instruction about literary elements as well as discussion during novel study or literature circles (30 minutes)	• Read aloud (15 minutes) • Shared reading (15 minutes) • Strategic reading groups, including independent reading and writing (35 minutes) • Word study (15 minutes)	• Read aloud (10 minutes) • Writing (40 minutes) • Literature study, including instruction about literary elements as well as discussion during novel study or literature circles (30 minutes)	• Read aloud (15 minutes) • Shared reading (15 minutes) • Strategic reading groups, including independent reading and writing (35 minutes) • Word study (15 minutes)

Table 2.3 Middle School Literacy Instruction, Traditional Class Periods (40 minutes each)

Monday	*Tuesday*	*Wednesday*	*Thursday*	*Friday*
Reading: • Shared reading (10 minutes) • Strategic reading groups, including independent reading and writing (30 minutes)	**Reading:** • Literature study, see Table 2.2 (30 minutes) • Read aloud (10 minutes)	**Reading:** • Shared reading (10 minutes) • Strategic reading groups, including independent reading and writing (30 minutes)	**Reading:** • Literature study (30 minutes) • Read aloud (10 minutes)	**Reading:** • Shared reading (10 minutes) • Strategic reading groups, including independent reading and writing (30 minutes)
Language Arts: • Writing (30 minutes) • Read aloud (10 minutes)	**Language Arts:** • Word study, vocabulary learning (10 minutes) • Strategic reading groups (30 minutes)	**Language Arts:** • Writing (30 minutes) • Read aloud (10 minutes)	**Language Arts:** • Word study, vocabulary learning (10 minutes) • Strategic reading groups (30 minutes)	**Language Arts:** • Writing (30 minutes) • Read aloud (10 minutes)

Table 2.4 Middle School Literacy Instruction, Language Arts Only (no reading, 40–60 minute periods)

Monday	Tuesday	Wednesday	Thursday	Friday
• Shared reading (10 minutes) • Strategic reading groups, including independent reading (15 minutes) • Writing (15–45 minutes)	• Literature study, see Table 2.2 (30 minutes) • Word study, vocabulary (10–15 minutes) • Read aloud (15–20 minutes)	• Shared reading (10 minutes) • Strategic reading groups, including independent reading (15 minutes) • Writing (15–45 minutes)	• Literature study (30 minutes) • Word study, vocabulary (10–15 minutes) • Read aloud (15–20 minutes)	• Shared reading (10 minutes) • Strategic reading groups, including independent reading (15 minutes) • Writing (15–45 minutes)

middle-level literacy instruction. While we are big fans of a block sched-ule (Table 2.2) for middle school literacy instruction, because teachers are able to spend large chunks of time on different areas of instruction and have more flexibility in their schedule, we know that many middle school teachers have separate periods for reading and language arts instruction (Table 2.3), while still others have only one period for language arts, without a period for reading instruction at all (Table 2.4). Regardless of the schedule, we still advocate for strategic reading groups, though the number of groups possible each week depends on the type of schedule teachers have. With a block schedule, we believe that teachers can work with six total groups each week by meeting with two groups, three times per week. This still leaves sufficient time for writing, word study, lit-erature study, and shared reading. For teachers in schools with separate reading and language arts periods, we believe that both the reading and language arts teachers should make time for strategic reading groups, with reading teachers seeing two groups, three times per week, and lan-guage arts teachers seeing two groups, twice a week.

Special consideration needs to be given to those schools that have only a single language arts period each day with no reading class (or reading instruction for only the most struggling students). It doesn't surprise us when teachers in such schools tell us that they can't possibly make time for strategic reading groups. Time constraints make it seem undoable. However, we believe unwaveringly that all middle school stu-dents, no matter what setting they are in, deserve the kind of individual-ized instruction that strategic reading groups uniquely provide. While teachers may not have time to meet with each group every week, they can still make time, three days per week, to meet with one group. In doing so, they can be assured of meeting with each of their groups every two weeks, while still attending to the other important features of balanced literacy instruction.

We also encourage teachers who only have one period of language arts instruction to work closely with their colleagues in the content areas. Perhaps the social studies and science teachers can each make time for independent reading once or more each week, in order to ensure that students have time to read self-selected independent-level books (in this case on topics germane to science or social studies cur-riculum). In addition, to supplement the limited time the language arts teacher has for reading aloud, content-area teachers should be encouraged to read aloud to their students, on topics that are relevant to their current area of instruction. There are plenty of examples of novels, picture books, and content-area trade books that would enrich content-area instruction in math, science, and social studies, while simultaneously allowing students to listen to and engage with great texts throughout their school day.

3

A Detailed Look at Strategic Reading Groups

Strategic grouping is an innovative middle school construct because of its emphasis on teacher feedback during individual students' oral reading. As students read on their own, teachers listen carefully and offer strategic cues to assist them in furthering their reading comprehension and vocabulary understanding. These kinds of ad hoc cues may be new to teachers, and they make the big difference in effecting change in student reading. Chapters 4, 5, and 6 are devoted to helping teachers understand and practice how to cue most effectively as students read in various genres. Before teachers are ready to work on the way they frame their cues, however, they need to be comfortable with the framework of the group, what students are doing as they sit in the groups, what the rest of the class is doing while the teacher is busy with this group, and what students are doing in between their cues.

This chapter breaks down the process into manageable steps. We suggest to teachers that they try this structure, and then figure out which parts do and do not work for them. There is no magic to the exact amount of time each segment takes except to the extent that the total time for the group should not exceed 15 minutes, which, in our experience, is about how long the rest of the class can engage productively in independent or paired literacy activities without teacher intervention. It is important that the students who are not in the group are not merely quiet and nondisruptive, but rather, that they are actually involved in authentic reading or writing. There is also nothing sacred about the way in which we start;

teachers may find another way works better for them while still maintaining the important components that we highlight.

As noted in our introductory chapter, we offer a field-tested model for strategic reading groups. The steps involved in the groups with approximate timing, repeated from Chapter 1, follow. After this overview, we explain each step, including examples of actual student and teacher interactions culled from transcripts gathered in middle school classrooms.

1. Teacher reminds students of the purpose of the group and of the necessity for the text to be a challenge (less than 30 seconds).

2. Teacher reminds students of a previously introduced strategy that may be useful for the difficulties ahead in this text (less than 30 seconds).

3. Teacher directs students to read silently (less than 30 seconds).

4. Teacher circulates to each student listening to them read until they miscue or demonstrate a comprehension breakdown. Teacher coaches each student through a strategy designed to help with the error.

5. Teacher moves to each student and repeats Step 4 (2 minutes per student, with about 5 students = 10 minutes).

6. Teacher asks students to stop reading and close their books (30 seconds).

7. Teacher helps students summarize the strategy they worked on with her and asks them to pay close attention to using the strategy for the rest of the day, in reading, as they study other subjects, and at home (2 minutes).

8. Teacher calls the next group and repeats Steps 1 through 7.

ELEMENTS OF SUCCESSFUL GROUPS

Step 1. Teacher reminds students of the purpose of the group and the necessity that the text is a challenge (less than 30 seconds).

One of the most difficult things for teachers to adjust to once they start working in these groups is selecting texts that will cause students to err quickly. It is counterintuitive for teachers to place texts in front of students that they believe they will not be able to read successfully. However, teachers quickly see the value in doing this, in picking just-slightly-too-difficult texts and the way it helps students learn to navigate increasingly difficult texts independently. It is worth it for the teacher to remind students, each time a groups gathers, that the text in front of them is one that the teacher selected particularly because it would be too difficult to understand without significant scaffolding. These groups are the only place in most students' days where they are able to work with a teacher one-on-one as they make meaning of texts. If students have no trouble making meaning in their one opportunity to read with the teacher that week, it is a missed chance for quality, customized instruction. It is important for teachers to make it clear to students that nobody can read everything with ease, and that even the most skilled readers confront texts that are a challenge. We find that beginning each group with this reminder is a good reinforcement of this idea. Here are some sample "launches" for this group process:

> I found this text when I was doing some research on my own and I thought it would be a good text with which to try to make meaning. Remember that I picked it because I thought it would be a good challenge, so don't feel worried if you struggle some; that is the idea.

Or,

> Okay, this is a section from your science book on the structure of cells. When Ms. Lawrence [the sixth-grade science teacher] gave me this, I read through and thought how confusing it was, so don't feel badly if you too are a little confused. Even Ms. Lawrence said she thought it was a challenge.

Step 2. Teacher reminds students of a previously introduced strategy that may be useful for the difficulties ahead in this text (less than 30 seconds).

As discussed in Chapter 2, strategic reading groups are one piece of instruction in a middle school literacy block, but there are many others. During some of these others, the whole group gets instruction in various strategies and processes for reading difficult texts. Teachers may want to remind students of one of these previously modeled and practiced strategies that they think might be helpful for the students in reading the text in front of them. A teacher should not, however, attempt to teach a new skill or strategy at the beginning of the group. Strategic reading groups aim to practice reading using strategies that a student has already been exposed to through other forms of instruction, thus revealing to the teacher where individual students need additional work on strategies, or what students may be ready for more advanced strategies or higher levels of texts. The teacher accomplishes this by working individually with each student in the group as she provides customized cues. In order for these groups to function optimally, each interaction must be kept brief; otherwise, there would be no time to teach the new strategies that need to be discussed and modeled in the whole group. It is also important to remember that students may have a wide variety of difficulty with a text that is beyond their comfort level. Some may be directed to use a strategy that had been discussed in class recently, while others may benefit from any number of other strategies that the teacher believes the students can handle with prompting and support. Thus, a teacher should not spend a good deal of time discussing a particular strategy, but merely remind students of a possible strategy. This 30-second (or less) comment may sound something like this:

> There are a lot of robust words in here, and some may be unfamiliar. Remember to look closely at the affixes to see if that might help you infer the meaning. Recall that I did that when I modeled my own reading the other day and encountered the word *immodestly*— remember that I looked at the prefix *im* and the suffix *ly* to help me figure out the word. That worked well in that instance.

Or,

> When I struggled with this, the science teacher suggested I look at the diagram before reading, so that is what I did and it helped. Give it a try.

Step 3. Teacher directs students to read silently (less than 30 seconds).

In years past, group work of this sort has been organized around a single student reading as the group listens. Research over the past twenty years has indicated that this "round-robin" reading is of no use. First, the attention placed on the students' reading pressures them and limits the cognitive space to really work on the task. Second, the students listening gain nothing from hearing a peer struggle through a text. Finally, students do not have the ability to know when is an appropriate time to cue or wait for peers to work out a reading difficulty on their own, and thus they jump in to correct their classmates before giving the reader an opportunity to invoke strategies that might be successful.

Strategic reading groups focus upon a single student reading to the teacher for a short time. While this student reads to the teacher, the rest of the students read the text silently, puzzling through their difficulties as best they can as they wait for the teacher. Once finished reading with the teacher, similarly, that student continues to read independently. The students understand that the text they are reading is difficult, and the teacher reiterates that they may struggle while awaiting the support she offers when she is able to listen.

Teachers often ask us if hearing a peer read aloud while they are reading silently distracts the other students. Our answer is yes and no. Many students get used to tuning out the other student as they read. Still others do not, and it is very common to see other students in the group simply watch and listen as the teacher works with their peer, while they wait.

We don't think this is of great help to the listening student, but we really don't see that it hurts anything. It is even possible that the student listening picks up on a suggestion that the teacher gives to another student. No matter, as long as students don't disrupt the work of the teacher–student pair, we think it is just fine. Right before the teacher begins her travels around the table to each student, she might say,

> Okay, now I want you all to read this text in silence until I get to you. If you struggle, do the best you can. Once I leave you, continue to practice until I stop everyone. When I get to you, just start reading aloud wherever you are in the text. I will catch up to you. However, I don't want you to be miserable while you wait, so if it is just too hard, simply pick up your independent reading book that I asked you to bring with you to the table and start reading that until I can get to you.

Step 4. Teacher moves to the first student, listening to this student read until the student miscues or demonstrates a comprehension breakdown. Teacher coaches student through a strategy designed to help with the error.

The real innovation in this kind of instruction is that each student's errors become the data the teacher uses to make on-the-fly instructional decisions. The teacher listens carefully to each student read, and in doing so, the teacher understands something about that student and the needs being demonstrated. In this short time, the teacher provides a single, customized cue that is drawn from the student's immediate needs. As the student reads, the teacher notices when there is a struggle and stops the student to discuss a possible strategy. It can sound something like the following exchange between Justin and his teacher, Mr. Sutton:

Justin: [reads aloud from a periodical about social networking] Social networking is the grouping of individuals into specific groups, like small, rural communities or a neighborhood subdivision, if you will.

Mr. Sutton: Okay, I am going to stop you there. To what are they comparing social networking? I want you to look up at me when you answer.

Justin: Um, like, a group?

Mr. Sutton: Hmm. It sounds like you need to read a little more specifically. Let's go back and look at that again, because I think the simile is lost if we don't think about it carefully and specifically as we read.

Justin: [reads aloud the same passage] They are comparing it to, like, a set of people, like people who live near each other and have things in common.

Mr. Sutton: Absolutely. That is well said. Okay, I want you to keep reading and remember that you want to really think about the text. Stop often and consider the meaning. Otherwise, you just gloss right over and don't really get what it is about. If you aren't going to get what reading is about, it is a poor use of time.

As this example illustrates, the brief interaction between teacher and student are the essence of the strategic reading groups. Mr. Sutton is highly skilled at listening to student reading and understanding what he hears. The skills involved in these teacher moves will be discussed in detail in Chapters 4, 5, and 6.

Step 5. Teacher moves to each student and repeats step 4 (2 minutes per student, with about 5 students = 10 minutes).

Once the teacher finishes with the first student, he moves on to the next. Most teachers elect to stand up and move to each of the students, kneeling next to them or pulling a chair close. Still others lean in to the student reading or ask the student to move toward them.

After he finishes with Justin, Mr. Sutton kneels down next to Sylvia, who is reading from the same periodical, but further down in the text:

Mr. Sutton: Can you begin right where you are and read aloud?

Sylvia: [reads aloud from text] This is because unlike most high schools, colleges, or workplaces, the Internet is filled with millions of individuals who are looking to meet other people, to gather and share first-hand information and experiences about cooking, golfing, gardening, developing friendships or professional alliances, finding employment, business-to-business marketing and even groups sharing information about the end of the Mayan calendar and the Great Shift to arrive December 21, 2012. The topics and interests are as varied and rich as the story of our world.

Mr. Sutton: Let's stop there. You seem to be running out of breath. It looks to me like that is a very long sentence. Look, it goes from here . . . [points to beginning] all the way to here. [points to end] There is no way to keep track of all that information at once, so let's think how we might chunk that sentence into parts. What do you think?

Sylvia: [looks down at text, then looks back at teacher]

Mr. Sutton: Why don't you listen to me read it and see what you hear. [reads aloud from same passage] This is because unlike most high schools, colleges, or workplaces, the Internet is filled with millions of individuals who are looking to meet other people, to gather and share first-hand information and experiences about . . .

I am going to stop right there for a minute because I see that they are about to create a list and I want to be sure I know what the list is capturing. Let's see, okay, I think they are going to list all the things you can do on the Internet and that makes sense to me since they are arguing for how many tons of people are using it. So now, I am going to read the list.

[reads aloud from text] . . . cooking, golfing, gardening, developing friendships or professional alliances, finding employment, business-to-business marketing and even groups sharing information about the end of the Mayan calendar and the Great Shift to arrive December 21, 2012. The topics and interests are as varied and rich as the story of our world.

Do you see how I prepared myself by stopping midsentence to kind of orient my thinking?

Sylvia: Yes.

Mr. Sutton: Okay, now I want you to read this next long sentence and see if you can come up with a place that you might stop and just sort of gather your thoughts. See what happens, okay? Let me hear you.

Sylvia: [reads next chunk, stopping midsentence]

Mr. Sutton: Much better! Do you see what you did? Do you see why? I am so impressed with how much you clearly understood that by reading it just a little differently. Keep thinking about that as you continue to read now, and later today.

Mr. Sutton then goes on to listen and cue the remaining three students.

Step 6. Teacher asks students to stop reading and close their books (30 seconds).

Once the teacher has had the opportunity to listen to the reading of each student, she asks students to finish up the sentence they are on and close their books. She might say:

When you finish the sentence you are reading right now, go ahead and stop reading and look at me.

Step 7. Teacher helps students summarize the strategy they worked on and asks them to pay close attention to using the strategy for the rest of the day, in reading, as they study other subjects, and at home (2 minutes).

The point of this type of reading instruction is for students to increase their ability to read independently. Anything they do in the company of the teacher should be invoked later when they are reading alone. It is worth it, thus, to take a little time to remind students of what they learned and to encourage them to practice this as they go through their reading day. The teacher may address each student separately, or combine advice with more than one student if they were cued similarly. Here is an example from Ms. Chen's seventh-grade classroom:

Ms. Chen: Please stop at the end of the next little bit of reading. You all did an excellent job on what I know was a very hard text. I am amazed at how much good work you did on it, as this would be hard even for an experienced adult reader. Mason, why don't you start and tell us what we worked on today?

Mason: You told me that sometimes, when you read something that you don't know very much about, that you look at the pictures, captions, tables, or charts first because it helps you know what it is going to be about.

Ms. Chen: Right, so what did we do?

Mason: We looked at the chart on the number of people in each country, so I knew it was going to be about that and that helped me.

Ms. Chen: Great, so later when you are reading in your social studies or science book, I want you to practice doing that even before you start reading and realize you might need it. Sara, can you tell us what we worked on?

Sara: Looking at parts of words that we don't know.

Ms. Chen: What word in particular?

Sara: We looked at the word *metropolis* and tried to think of what the two parts might be.

Ms. Chen: That is right, and we struggled, didn't we? We broke it up into *metro* and *polis* and then discovered we didn't know those words either, but it is still a really good strategy because sometimes you will. I figured out that the word *metro* is sort of like city, so that would have helped me and sometimes the words will help you as well. Good. Liam, how about you? Actually, you read it fine, at least the part that I heard, so unfortunately, we didn't get any strategy practice, but I want you to listen to the friends around you and see what you hear about what they learned. Kyle?

Kyle: I was reading too quickly and you said that I should slow down and think about what I was reading at the end of each sentence.

Ms. Chen: Yep, we can all stand to be reminded of that. Now I want you all to look me in the eye and promise to try to remember that when you are reading things that are pretty simple or enjoyable or for pleasure, just read. However, when you are reading tough things, things that might be unfamiliar or have words you haven't seen before, that you have to do something, something to give yourself a chance to understand. There is no reason to just plow through reading without understanding.

As Ms. Chen's dialogue with her students illustrates, it is so important to help students understand the role of strategic reading, when it is helpful, how sometimes even good strategies aren't helpful, and to remind them that the learning they do inside the group should leave the group with them. Teachers often write these strategies on a sticky note (or ask students to write them down) for students to place on their desks or in their reading folders as a prompt. Others give students blank bookmarks that they can write on as they accumulate strategies. The teacher will often take notes for herself about what strategies she worked on with each student. These notes can be helpful if students cannot recall the strategy they worked on during the group.

When we model these groups in classrooms, teachers are often surprised at the power of these last few minutes of the group. The ability of students to put the reading strategies they worked on into their own words often suggests a deeper understanding of the strategies than teachers expect, and also serves as a useful reinforcement for every student in the group.

Step 8. Teacher calls the next group and repeats Steps 1 through 7.

As we discussed in the last chapter, middle school teachers often set the goal of seeing two groups per day. Once this group disbands, we recommend that the teacher take 5 minutes to pull the whole class back together either to redirect activities for the next portion of time when he has another group, or sometimes just to break up the time by doing a brief read aloud or other pleasurable literacy activity. It takes some middle school students great effort to concentrate long enough to manage themselves without the teacher's presence. It is sometimes a bit of a relief to be teacher managed for a few minutes.

PULLING THE PIECES TOGETHER

Teachers can adjust the details and exact timing as they see fit. As the discussion in this chapter indicates, the really important part, the part that sets these groups apart from others in which most teachers have worked, is the specific kind of student–teacher interaction, outlined previously and discussed in depth in the chapters to follow.

4

Listening to Fluent Readers

It is not difficult to tell when a beginning reader is struggling. One must only listen to a developing reader to know that there has been a word-level miscue: an omission of a word, a substitution of a word, or an addition of a word. Teachers of young children listen carefully to hear these kinds of miscues. Fluent readers, however, mask their reading struggles. We have all run into students who read every word beautifully, yet cannot summarize what they have read or pick out important concepts. This practice, often known as *word calling,* seems like reading to some, and many students believe full well that visually registering and then verbally articulating accurate text is effective reading. Literacy educators and researchers believe, however, that the goal of reading is *meaning making* and thus, anything short of that does not constitute reading. It is likely that one of the reasons teachers do not privilege listening to students read aloud once they are able decoders is that they don't know what to listen for. If students pronounce words and read full sentences coherently, it may not feel like a good use of time to listen carefully. Our experience, however, suggests that once teachers know how to listen to fluent readers, this listening becomes a crucial tool for both assessment and instruction. As mentioned in Chapter 1, our work with K–5 readers influenced our work on strategic reading groups. Once these students were reading fluently, we noticed teachers beginning to listen carefully for clues about their comprehension and vocabulary knowledge as revealed through their individual, oral reading. As we worked with these teachers, we noted how much progress even the highest upper elementary readers were making with this support, and decided to test the model with middle grade readers. We ran into little reluctance on the part of the students, who, similar to the elementary students we worked with, really appreciated the opportunity to have their teachers' undivided attention for even a short time, as they worked on improving their use of reading strategies. We did find teachers resistant to the idea, and the more we pursued it, the more we understood that they had had little training and experience in listening to students reading aloud.

As noted in earlier chapters, the point of the group is the teacher–student interactions. As a student reads aloud, a knowledgeable teacher listens carefully to understand what a student can and cannot do. The brief discussion following this oral reading confirms the teacher's interpretation of the reading and is the site for individualized, scaffolded instruction. In this chapter, we will discuss just this first point—hearing the student read and making reasonable inferences about individual meaning-making abilities and struggles based on that reading. We believe that this careful listening can provide us with a meaningful assessment of student reading that can lead to wise and differentiated instructional decision making—the kinds of teacher moves shown repeatedly to foster student reading.

STUDENT READING AND TEACHER RESPONSE

When fluent readers read aloud, there are a number of clues that can indicate they are not understanding what they read. Paying close attention to the way students read the text helps the teacher determine breakdowns in comprehension, and often determine why those breakdowns are occurring. In strategic reading groups, it is important to tune into when these breakdowns occur, as they present the perfect place for instruction. When students' oral reading demonstrates a meaning lapse, we say that the students are "asking" for the instruction that they need. Instead of the teacher coming in with an agenda for what is to be taught, the learners set the agenda by demonstrating what they are and are not able to do. Once a teacher recognizes that a student is not making appropriate meaning, the teacher can coach that student with a strategy that they can try together on the spot. We will discuss what to say to coach students on particular meaning breakdowns in Chapters 5 and 6. For now, we focus on recognizing when something has gone awry in students' reading.

Before going on to list the aspects of student reading that often indicate something gone wrong, consider this example from Mrs. Andrews's fifth-grade classroom. Henry is reading from an informational text called *Dancing Bees* by M. Facklam (1992):

Henry: When a honeybee discovers a rich supply of nectar, it
                    flies back to the hive to tell the other bees exactly where

the food is, and how good it is. How can an insect with a brain no bigger than a grass seed describe all this information? Dr. Karl Von Frisch was the first person to find out. He would put a dot of red dye on a worker bee and watched as she flew off and returned to the hive. (p.13)

Mrs. Andrews: Okay, I am going to stop you there. I hear that you are pronouncing all the words accurately—they aren't that hard, right? They are mostly words that are familiar to you and you know.

Henry: [nods]

Mrs. Andrews: But you were reading it so fast that I could barely follow you. Do you think you were following your own reading?

Henry: [shrugs]

Mrs. Andrews: I think we need to find out because it does nobody any good to say the words, even if you say them accurately, if you aren't putting any meaning to them. Then they are just sounds and it is kind of a waste of your time. So I am going to ask you, without looking back at the text, do you know what the scientist was trying to find out?

Henry: Something about bees?

Mrs. Andrews: Well, yes, but we could tell that just based on the title. What was he trying to find out about the bees?

Henry: Where they are going?

Mrs. Andrews: Hmm. That feels like a question rather than a statement, so I think we just learned that we aren't really sure and that we probably shouldn't go on until we are. I know that it feels like it takes time to go back and figure out what you do and do not understand, but really if you don't you will never have any understanding, and then the whole reading will have been wasted. I am going to give you a strategy that I sometimes use when I realize I am reading along and don't know exactly what is going on in the text. I tend to stop and just underline some key words. Remember when I was modeling my own reading about the bacteria found in the food in those fancy restaurants the other day, and I decided to underline the parts that told me how to figure out what was and was not clean? What if you did something like that and went back and underlined when you were told what the scientists were trying to determine? Can you try that with my pen and see what happens?

Henry: Sure.

Much is going on in this brief exchange. First, Mrs. Andrews praises Henry and checks in with him about his impression of the reading. Next, she points out that she struggled to follow the meaning because of the pace of his reading. She does this because it is accurate, but also because she wants Henry to recognize that reading challenging texts quickly often causes meaning breakdown. Next, she asks Henry a question, even though she is fairly sure he cannot answer it, because she wants him to notice that meaning has not been made in any robust way. After this, she calls attention to what Henry has done and reminds him of a strategy that she has already modeled for the whole class. Finally, she asks him to try that strategy to see if it helps him build more coherent meaning of the text. All this occurs within a couple minutes, and then Mrs. Andrews moves on to the same type of interaction with the next student. While this student may or may not reveal the same needs, it is likely that a similar kind of conversation will take place. Table 4.1 lists the components of this conversation. Like many of the parts of the group instruction, it is helpful to have a chart like this at hand when a teacher is just getting started with group instruction.

This chapter looks carefully at Steps 1 through 5, while the next two chapters detail and discuss Steps 6 and 7. The following section centers upon a few common clues for which teachers can listen that often indicate a meaning breakdown or incoherence in textual understanding. We have found that teachers are relieved to know that many of these clues are easy to recognize and really are good indications that students need some reading support.

Table 4.1   Teacher Instructional Moves

1. Teacher listens to student read.

2. Teacher hears something that may indicate a meaning breakdown.

3. Teacher asks student to stop reading.

4. Teacher says what she notices.

5. Teacher determines if meaning indeed has broken down.

6. Teacher offers student a strategy.

7. Teacher asks student to practice the strategy.

STANDARDS OF COHERENCE

Often, a teacher will suspect that a student isn't making meaning, yet the student clearly believes she is. This is what van den Broek and Kremer (2000) refer to as a "low standard of coherence." They explain that students, especially struggling students, are so accustomed to not understanding what they read, or understanding it only on the most superficial level, that they don't know how to demand more from their reading. In contrast, strong readers know that texts should make full and clear meaning and if they don't, these students keep working at them.

The following example illustrates how *standards of coherence* guide a strong reader's meaning making:

> Claudia learns that her sister has an ailment that she doesn't know much about. In order to learn more, she goes online and reads a bunch of medical reports on that ailment. Some of this medical reading is out of her comfort zone and, thus, she struggles to understand. Because she is concerned about her sister, Claudia doesn't want to settle for understanding only the most basic level of what this ailment is and how it will affect her sister. Instead, she uses strategies such as rereading, highlighting, and taking notes to dig out the complexity of the text, and she doesn't stop until she feels that she has enough understanding to be able to answer her most pressing questions. This indicates that Claudia has a high standard of coherence, that is, a high demand for making sense of complexity. She doesn't understand every nuance, but when she finds herself facing challenging text that confuses her, even with the use of strategies, she says to herself, "Well, clearly I don't understand this and maybe I need to talk with someone before I continue to try to learn about this through reading."

As a strong reader, Claudia had high expectations for her meaning making. She knew when she didn't understand, and she had strategies in place to help make sense of the text. Many of our students, on the other hand, will read and gain enough understanding to answer the most general of questions, but they won't recognize that their understanding is partial or tentative. Henry, presented earlier, in reading about bees, knew enough to answer questions very generally, but he could not say anything about the more complicated concepts. If his standard of coherence were higher, he might have known that he really had no idea what the passage was saying beyond the most general parts.

Because students often haven't been taught to demand a lot from their reading, they will believe that a very general answer is sufficient. Our goal in scaffolding student comprehension through our attention to their oral reading is to get them to push themselves to make complicated and total meaning from difficult texts. We want them to understand that one- or two-word answers in response to questions about text are not sufficient, and if that is all we are going to ask of ourselves, reading the title or just the section heading would be sufficient. In strategic reading groups, we choose texts specifically so that our students can begin to understand what it really means to make sense of challenging texts, and how to notice when they have not done so.

WHAT TO LISTEN FOR IN STUDENT READING

There are several common indicators that students are reading, yet not understanding. These can suggest a vocabulary deficit related to the particular text, a lack of use of vocabulary strategies, or a lack of comprehension not related to individual word understanding. Student reading behaviors indicating a good probability that a student is struggling to make meaning include the following four categories: (1) pace, (2) prosody, (3) punctuation, and (4) pushing through miscues. Because these all are conveniently identified by the letter *P*, we use the term *4 Ps* as a memory jog for teachers. When a teacher hears any of the 4 Ps or some combination of two or more, it is a signal to stop and determine if the student is doing what it takes to gather enough meaning from the text. Each P is discussed subsequently and followed by a brief example culled from our tapes of middle school teachers working with their students. Because of the difficulty of representing the way students read in a transcript, we present just the text. Preceding each example, we note the way in which the student is reading. Instead of trying to represent this with a series of intricate markings, we ask readers to draw on their own experience listening to students reading to imagine the nature of the oral reading.

Pace. As in the example on bees, the most common indicator that a student is reading without appropriate and full understanding is pace of reading. While it is, of course, true that some students are naturally slower or faster in their pace, a teacher knows when a student is reading too quickly for meaning making of challenging text. It isn't always a quick pace, however, that is the problem. When students read very laboriously and slowly it may be because they are sounding words out (a great cognitive tax that leaves little room for comprehension to occur simultaneously) or are reading words that they can decode but may not understand. Students who read uncharacteristically quickly or slowly are likely not comprehending sufficiently.

As an example of a student reading at too fast a speed was presented earlier, here is an example of an eighth-grade teacher, Mrs. De Rosa, listening to her student, Kayla, read very slowly from an article by Diane Ravitch (2010) about educational policy. Note that the student pronounces every word correctly, so there are no audible decoding or word recognition errors:

Kayla:	The theory behind NCLB was that schools would improve dramatically if every child in Grades 3 to 8 were tested every year and the results made public. Texas did exactly this, and advocates claimed it had seen remarkable results: test scores went up, the achievement gap between students of different races was closing, and graduation rates rose. At the time, a few scholars questioned the claims of a "Texas miracle," but Congress didn't listen.
Mrs. De Rosa:	I'm going to stop you there because I noticed you reading more slowly and less fluently than usual. You didn't mispronounce any words, but your slow pace suggested to me that either the words or the concepts were unfamiliar to you. There is absolutely nothing wrong with reading a difficult text slowly—don't misunderstand. But something about the way you were reading made me think you were struggling a little.

Mrs. De Rosa goes on to coach Kayla on some of the words and ideas that were indeed unfamiliar and caused the slowness of the oral reading.

Prosody. Literacy researchers and teachers use the word *prosody* to describe some combination of inflection, variation in pacing, and expression that shows good fluency and is often an indicator of capable self-monitoring and, thus, good comprehension. When any one of these characteristics is absent—proper pacing, expression, or inflection—it is of concern. Often, all three suffer, resulting in the very flat-toned oral reading that is characteristic of very young readers. Word-by-word reading, which lacks vocal modulation and appropriate pausing and pace changes, is often associated with word calling. Like pace, prosody can vary greatly in readers. Some students are naturally more dramatic in their oral reading and others more monotone. Yet, a teacher should note if the prosody is uncharacteristic for the student at hand, and if it is, wonder about the comprehension as the teacher does in the following illustration. In this example, sixth grader Thomas is reading aloud to his teacher Mrs. Wood, from an essay by Sam Anderson (2011) titled, "What I Really Want Is Someone Rolling Around in the Text."

Thomas:	One day in college I was trawling the library for a good book to read when I found a book called *How to Read a Book*. I tried to read it, but must have been doing something wrong, because it struck me as old-fashioned and dull, and I could get through only a tiny chunk of it. That chunk, however, contained a statement that changed my reading life forever. The author argued that you didn't truly own a book (spiritually, intellectually) until you had marked it up. (p. 46)

Mrs. Wood:	Let's go ahead and stop reading there. Listening carefully to you, I noticed that your reading sounded . . . a . . . little . . . flat [speaks in a rote, slow, mechanized way mimicking the manner in which the student just read]. When I find myself reading that way, it is often because I am just looking at the words and saying them. I know when I assign meaning to words that the pace of my reading varies, that my voice rises and falls, and that certain sentences are said with more emphasis. Because you weren't doing that and you often do, I am wondering if you are getting the depth of meaning here that you will need to make meaning as you continue to read.

Mrs. Wood goes on to model her own oral reading of the passage and coaches Thomas in listening for when he finds himself reading very mechanistically.

Punctuation. Part of prosody and pace can be attention or inattention to punctuation, but it is so common when students aren't self-monitoring that it merits special attention. When students don't stop at periods or commas, or stop not long enough, they are often getting tangled in the text. Similarly, when students stop at ends of lines or other places in the text where there is no end punctuation, we know something is likely interfering with meaning. In the next example, Mr. Henderson works with Lucas, who is reading an excerpt from a Bill Bryson (2000) essay in which he pokes fun at any sport that isn't baseball.

Lucas:	I'm joking, of course. Cricket is a wonderful sport, full of deliciously scattered micromoments of real action. If a doctor ever instructs me to take a complete rest and not get overexcited, I shall become a fan at once. In the meantime, my heart belongs to baseball. It's what I grew up with, what I played as a boy, and that of course is vital to any meaningful appreciation of a sport. I had this brought home to me many years ago in England when I went out on a soccer ground with a couple of British friends to knock a ball around. (p. 16)

Mr. Henderson:	Bill Bryson is so funny. I think I am having a little trouble getting all of the humor because the sentence breaks were a little awkward. I noticed that you weren't always stopping for a full breath at the periods, or any breath at all at the commas. When there is a lot of dense text like this, that is really helpful in organizing your reading. Can you give it a try as you continue to read? Listen as I do it.

Mr. Henderson goes on to model his own oral reading of the passage and coaches Lucas in what to do if he finds himself reading past punctuation, or stopping at the ends of lines instead of end punctuation.

Pushing through miscues. With elementary readers, we talk a lot about self-correction and miscues. When a beginning reader sees the line *The boy bounced the ball* and reads it as *The boy bunked the ball,* we wait to see if the student will go back to the beginning of the sentence and try it again. If the student is closely monitoring his reading, he will understand that the sentence did not make sense and attempt a reread. If the student keeps going, we can infer that he is not using meaning cues to help decode an unknown word. We can do the same with older readers. When students mispronounce familiar words or struggle to decode unfamiliar words, we know something about their monitoring systems.

Here, a sixth-grade reader, Nina, attempts a difficult passage from a scientific text on calculating glycemic index (NutritionData.com, n.d.):

Nina:	The glycemic index is a numerical index that ranks carbohydrates based on their rate of glycemic response (i.e., their conversion to glucose within the human body). Glycemic index uses a scale of 0 to 100, with higher values given to foods that cause the most rapid rise in blood sugar. Pure glucose serves as a reference point, and is given a glycemic index (GI) of 100. (para. 1)
Mrs. Carter:	I hear that you are stumbling. I know that we talked about knowing that some words don't really need to be understood in order to understand a whole passage, but you know that some do. I heard that you stumbled over this one [points to *glycemic*], this one [points to *carbohydrates*] and this one [points to *conversion*] . . . With all those difficulties, it would be nearly impossible to get any deep meaning from the passage. I think we should go back and see if we can use our vocabulary strategies to figure out some of these tricky words.

Because Nina clearly did not know the vocabulary she was pronouncing, yet did not stop to work through the words, it was clear to Mrs. Carter that Nina was not self-monitoring closely enough. When students read through mispronunciations, omissions, or additions, and these miscues violate the meaning of the passage, it is clear that students aren't holding to a standard of coherence high enough for appropriate meaning making. This is when the teacher intervenes and offers a cue. The following two chapters discuss appropriate cues for information and narrative texts.

5

Teacher Cueing During Informational Text Reading

Here, Alex reads a section about remote control units out of David Macaulay's (1998) informational text, *The New Way Things Work*, while his teacher, Mrs. Simon, listens:

Alex:	The receiver unit contains a photodiode, which is a diode sensitive to light or infra-red rays. It is connected in reverse bias so that normally only a low current flows through it. When rays strike the diode, they free some electrons, increasing the current to produce a signal which goes to the decoder. (p. 272)
Mrs. Simon:	Can you tell me what you just learned about the receiver unit in a remote control?
Alex:	Honestly, I don't know.
Mrs. Simon:	Can you read it again? This time, after every sentence, I want you to pause and put it in your own words. This is technical and dense so you will need to do that to keep track of what you are reading.

Mrs. Simon notices one of the four Ps discussed in the previous chapter, *prosody*. Alex was reading in a severe monotone, not inflecting or pausing appropriately. Because she heard that, she stopped his reading and prepares to intervene.

In the previous chapter, we talked about the clues (pace, prosody, punctuation, and pushing through miscues) that might indicate students are struggling to make meaning. In this chapter, we talk about how to find out if those clues actually do reveal misreadings, and then how to help students use strategies to make meaning of the text in front of them. This chapter focuses on informational text. The next chapter takes up the same topics when working with narrative texts.

QUESTIONS TO ASK

Teachers generally keep a small repertoire of questions (Table 5.1) that they use when stopping students to gauge their understanding. These questions need not be complicated, because eventually we want students to moderate their own reading, asking themselves the same kinds of questions. The questions should be simple, yet teachers should demand much of the answers. It would be all too easy for Mrs. Simon to ask about the above passage on remote control units: "What was the passage about?" and for Alex to say, "remote control units." Though this may be true, it can easily be gleaned by just the title. We want students to sink into reading that challenges them, not gloss over it, which is why Mrs. Simon was intentional in asking Alex what he knew about a particular aspect of the passage.

One caution that we can offer after doing this with dozens of middle school students: teachers also have to concentrate and activate their strategies in order to make meaning of texts. At times, we will ask a student a question and then realize that we aren't sure of the answer ourselves. When we notice this, we say, "You know, I am not sure either. Let's go back together and do something so we can figure out the answer, and let's notice what we do as we try."

Teachers can usually gather enough meaning from elementary school texts without having to fully concentrate on them, but not so for middle grade student reading, which becomes increasingly more complex.

Table 5.1   Questions to Discern Deep Understanding

What did you just learn about XYZ (e.g., the digestive system, Helen Keller, the American West)?

What do you think the next section will cover?

Can you summarize the most important detail that you just read?

How does this paragraph connect to the previous one?

In some cases, we lose focus ourselves and are unable to come up with a reasonably specific question. In that case, we just ask the student to reread. Suffice it to say that doing this kind of work with students demands teacher concentration. This is why, as we discuss in Chapter 9, it is so important to make sure the rest of the class remains productively engaged in independent literacy activities, so that we can focus all of our attention on the strategic reading group in front of us. Teachers simply cannot worry about other students as they try to focus on a particular student reader.

The very skilled teachers we have watched are adept at noticing something about student reading, asking a question like those in Table 5.1 to confirm their hunch that the student did not understand, and then listening carefully to the student's answer.

At times, the teacher will have misinterpreted the reason for the student reading difficulty. It isn't *always* true that these indicators reveal true misunderstandings. If the text the teacher selected is within a student's independent reading level and is not even a modest struggle, the student may very well be able to read without much inflection, or may be able to read quite quickly and still make significant meaning. Perhaps it isn't a comprehension breakdown at all. If this is the case and the student indeed does answer the query appropriately, the teacher might help that student draw attention to the strategies she did use, as the teacher in the next example demonstrates. Kate, an eighth-grade student, is reading an article out of a local newspaper on legislation that would further limit the number of pets permitted in a given single residence. Kate is reading quite quickly, so her teacher, Mrs. Mendoza, stops and asks one of the questions listed in Table 5.1.

Mrs. Mendoza: Can you tell me what you just learned about the proposed legislation?

Kate: They are saying that you can only have two dogs over 75 pounds or three dogs that together weigh a certain amount, or else it is considered a pound or animal shelter and that is zoned commercially.

Mrs. Mendoza: I think that is right. You understood that really well even though it was a hard read and you went over it quickly. Do you know what you did in order to make meaning so accurately?

Kate: I am interested in this because I have a dog and want another one, so I guess I just was interested.

Mrs. Mendoza: That is a good point. When we are interested, we tend to understand better. When we aren't interested, one of the jobs of a good reader is to make ourselves become interested. Great work.

Strategic reading groups are best used as sites for coaching and practice, yet at times students do just fine without our help. Mrs. Mendoza notes that Kate used a strategy well and will attempt to pick a text for next time that will cause a greater struggle.

ATTENDING BREAKDOWNS AND MEANING BREAKDOWNS

Once we have a hunch that a reader is not fully comprehending (as discussed in Chapter 4), and have confirmed that hunch with a question (discussed in the previous section), we want to offer students a strategy for making meaning of the difficult text. All readers have the experience of reading through a text and at some point being struck with the realization that they have no idea what they just read. In the real adult world of self-selected readings, this may result in one of two things. Many times, the adult reader decides that the thing she was reading is not of enough interest to sustain her, and so she merely abandons it for another pursuit. At other times, an adult reader is motivated enough for the task (because it is for his job or to solve a problem or some other compelling reason), so that he goes back and uses a strategy to help himself pay attention. Sometimes that is merely saying to himself, "Hey, this is important and this time around I am going to pay very strict attention." Other times, he might intentionally activate a strategy like summarizing small chunks or underlining. In either case, adult readers rededicate themselves to understanding the text in front of them. Very often, for good readers, this second decision to actively invoke a strategy for attending to the text results in appropriate meaning making.

Other times, though, even this overt attention to the reading process can result in misunderstandings. There are just some texts that are too hard for some readers. The difficulty in understanding them may be due to a lack of background knowledge on the topic (i.e., it would be hard to understand the infield fly rule if one didn't understand the rules of baseball); it may be due to conceptual misunderstandings (i.e., it would be hard to understand laws of probability without a basic understanding of randomness and mathematical certainty); it may be due to unfamiliar vocabulary (i.e., a medical insurance claim may be hard to discern because of unknown terminology). If any or some combination of these are indeed the case, all the rereading in the world, even rereading ripe with excellent strategies, may not do the job. For these kind of meaning breakdowns, another set of strategies are often invoked.

We call the first kind of reading breakdown a breakdown in *attending* and the second one a breakdown in *meaning*. In the first case, the text is within the readers' ability once they focus and do something to actively engage with the text. In the second, all the engagement in the world may still result in partial or no understanding. One of the important skills that students can gain from comprehension instruction is acknowledging the difference between the two. We encourage teachers to help students see when they struggle because of attention and when they struggle because of meaning. We also teach students that attending breakdowns are not caused by laziness or lack of trying.

All readers have trouble attending sometimes, when texts are particularly difficult or readers are not engaged in the texts, or readers are fatigued. It isn't a sign of attention deficit disorder or the like; it isn't even a sign of poor reading. All readers struggle with attention at times; it is just that good readers recognize that they are struggling. Recall from the discussion in the previous chapter that often students have a very low standard of coherence. Because many of their reading experiences have resulted in very low levels of understanding, they don't always expect reading to make sense. Thus, when they finish a passage that they have read but not assigned meaning to, they may not be particularly bothered. It is our instructional task to get them to see what they have and have not done.

In order to reinforce the difference between a meaning breakdown and an attention breakdown, we ask students to look at a chart like that found in Figure 5.1 and practice using it as they read something that is difficult.

Figure 5.1   Comprehension Breakdown Chart

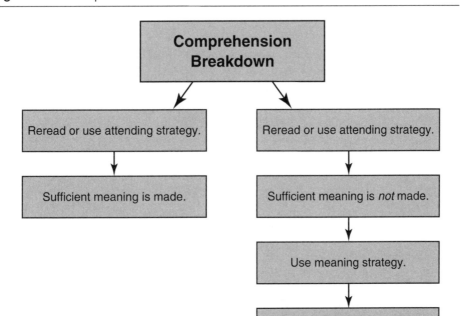

As Figure 5.1 illustrates, students go through a process whereby they must tangle with their own reading to determine whether they did or did not understand.

Attending cues. Because attending cues result from not assigning meaning to words or phrases, the goals of cueing for attention are to direct the reader to the task at hand in very explicit ways. It is worth repeating that not attending is not a character or behavioral flaw, it is a matter of reading strategies. Our students often do not attend because they lack strategies for attending to that which doesn't interest them or is very difficult. Because this is the case, teaching them a strategy for attending to a particular text may not help them attend to another. The need to cue for attending will likely come up again and again during strategic reading groups and will be repeated and reinforced throughout high-quality reading instruction.

Table 5.2 lists a number of attending cues for informational texts. Following the chart, the cues are elaborated and examples of students and teachers working with these cues offered.

Table 5.2   Powerful Attending Cues for Informational Text

Go back and reread.

Reread in smaller portions.

Ask a question after each sentence or small set of sentences.

Take notes on or highlight text.

Summarize small pieces.

Reread. Sometimes it is as simple as reminding oneself to pay attention on a second read. Notice how the teacher, Mr. Potter, in the next example, uses a question discussed in Chapter 4 to determine that his seventh-grade student, Edgar, has not understood, and then prompts Edgar with an attending cue. On a second try, Edgar is successful. He is reading from an online government document produced by FEMA (2010):

Edgar: Floodplain management is the operation of a community program of corrective and preventative measures for reducing flood damage. These measures take a variety of forms and generally include requirements for zoning, subdivision or building, and special-purpose floodplain ordinances. A community's agreement to adopt and enforce floodplain management ordinances, particularly with respect to new construction, is an important element in making flood insurance available to home and business owners. Currently over 20,100 communities voluntarily adopt and enforce local floodplain management ordinances that provide flood loss reduction building standards for new and existing development. (para. 1)

Mr. Potter: Can you tell me what the relationship between flood-plain management and flood insurance is?

Edgar: Not really.

Mr. Potter: I think that may be because you weren't concentrating on the text deeply enough. Primary source documents are hard that way because they often have raw data that isn't prettied up for readers. Nonetheless, it is important that if we are going to read it, we read it well.

In this example, Mr. Potter must believe that the text will make sense to Edgar if he attends carefully. Mr. Potter intentionally does not offer a strategy beyond "reread" because he doesn't think Edgar will need anything further. On a second read, Mr. Potter proves correct. After Edgar reads the text again, Mr. Potter notes that he has slowed his oral reading down significantly.

Mr. Potter: Now what do you think is the relationship between floodplain management and flood insurance?

Edgar: If people manage the floodplains they can get insurance.

Mr. Potter: Seems that way. Well done on that second reading.

Other attending cues. At times, merely rereading will not be enough support for students to make deep meaning out of a text. In these cases, teachers draw upon strategies that they themselves use when they confront texts difficult to understand without strategic reading. As discussed in an earlier chapter, these strategies are often ones that the teacher has modeled in a whole group mini-lesson; thus, students will be familiar with the strategy. Small group instruction like the kind described in this book is seldom the place for introduction of new ideas. Instead, it is a place for a teacher to help a student apply a strategy previously studied. The teacher in the next example helps a student by reminding her of a whole group lesson and then modeling the strategy for the student before having her try it independently. The fifth grader is reading an article about Alexander the Great from *Junior Scholastic* (Brown, 2011).

Maggie: Alexander seemed destined for greatness early on. Strikingly handsome, the prince was a superb athlete, hunter, and horseman. He was tutored by the famous Greek philosopher Aristotle, and revered Greek culture. Even as a boy, Alexander was fearless. No one else could

> tame the giant horse Bucephalus, but he succeeded. "My son, Macedonia is too small for you," his father is said to have told him. "Seek out a larger empire worthier of you." (p. 20)

Mrs. Rosario: Do you know much about Alexander the Great?

Maggie: Not really.

Mrs. Rosario: I wonder if you can tell me what you think the most important part of the passage you just read might be.

Maggie: That his father tutored him with Aristotle?

Mrs. Rosario: His father?

Maggie: Yes.

Mrs. Rosario: I think we could think more about this, but we are going to have to read much less at once. Remember the other day when I was reading in front of the class and I read that *Wall Street Journal* article on the economy? I was having so much trouble following it that I stopped after every sentence and just checked myself. By doing this, I was able to figure out what I did and did not understand. Listen to how I might do it with this text, how I check my understanding as I go along.

> [reads aloud from text] Alexander seemed destined for greatness early on.
> Okay I understand that. I am going to keep going.
> [reads aloud from text] Strikingly handsome, the prince was a superb athlete, hunter, and horseman.
> They are saying that he was all around amazing, good at everything.
> [reads aloud from text] He was tutored by the famous Greek philosopher Aristotle, and revered Greek culture.
> His teacher was Aristotle, whom I know was very famous and they are also saying that he learned a lot about and appreciated Greek art, music, literature and maybe even food and religion. All of that can be part of culture.
> Do you see how I checked myself?

Maggie: Yes.

Mrs. Rosario: Now I want you to read the rest of the passage just that way. I know it takes longer, but it doesn't help to read fast without understanding.

Teachers work with students on attending cues like this to give students ideas about what they might do to force their own attention and to self-monitor. The point is always to increase students' ability to discern their own understanding, and, when they note it isn't complete enough, to use something from their toolbox to help move their understanding along.

Meaning cues. At times, all the attention in the world to a text will still not result in appropriate meaning making. When students are attending (i.e., monitoring their own understanding), but still note that they cannot comprehend the text, we offer meaning cues. These strategies help students to better understand the words, sentences, and ideas presented in a text. Table 5.3 lists some of the key meaning strategies. It is worth noting that there are some texts that will simply not yield to any strategy. For nearly every reader, there will be a time when confronted with a text that the reader simply cannot understand. Students should be told this, so that they do not panic or give up merely because strategies fail once or twice. The more that readers use strategies to make meaning of texts that are a bit too hard, the greater their ability to read more and more difficult texts.

As Table 5.3 illustrates, meaning cues can be generally classified into two categories. The first relates to comprehension strategies. These strategies go beyond attending cues because they must help students access information or use unfamiliar data. In the next example, Mrs. Bremwall uses two of the three strategies in the comprehension category with her sixth graders, one with Cassie and one with Owen.

The students are reading from an interview with Paul Chappell, a former army captain who served in Iraq and later wrote the book *Will War*

Table 5.3   Powerful Meaning Cues for Informational Text

Comprehension Cues
- Activate background knowledge.
- Use text features.
- Access another source.

Vocabulary Cues
- Use vocabulary analysis strategies: prefixes, suffixes, roots, cognates.
- Use context of sentence or paragraph.

Ever End? A Soldier's Vision of Peace for the 21st Century. The author, Leslee Goodman (2011), asks Chappell a series of questions. Students read the interview as Mrs. Bremwall circulates:

Cassie:	West Point teaches that war is so dangerous it should be used only as a last resort. I learned that the United States needs to rely more on diplomacy, that politicians don't understand war and are too quick to use it as a means of conflict resolution. West Point also teaches that if you want to understand war, you have to understand its limitations and unpredictability.
Mrs. Bremwall:	Do you understand what he is saying about what he learned about war?
Cassie:	Not really. I am not sure what West Point is and what it has to do with anything.
Mrs. Bremwall:	Well, what is one thing you can do when you don't know a reference?
Cassie:	Try to figure it out?
Mrs. Bremwall:	Yes, so what can you do to try to figure it out?
Cassie:	Use the context?
Mrs. Bremwall:	Okay, does the context help?
Cassie:	Not really.
Mrs. Bremwall:	Sometimes it does, sometimes it does not. I think in this case we might need to do some further inquiry. You could go to the Internet, or look in another book, but this time I am just going to tell you that West Point is an institute of higher education that trains men and women to be army officers. So does that help?
Cassie:	I guess he is saying that when he was in school he learned that war is the last resort.
Mrs. Bremwall:	Right. Very good. Finding out one thing helped you make meaning of the whole thing. I want you to remember that. I am going to move along to another student. I want you to keep reading and think about the fact that sometimes one piece of information leads you to understandings.

Okay, Owen, why don't you start reading aloud from where you are.

Owen: I'm not sure that the Iraq War is just about oil, but I think most people will agree that if there were not a single drop of oil in the Middle East, we would not be over there. (p. 5)

Mrs. Bremwall: Before you go on, I want you to think about what you already know about the Iraq War from things you have read or discussed with your parents, in class, anywhere. This will help you to understand better what this man is arguing about.

Owen: Should I tell you?

Mrs. Bremwall: You can, but if it is more comfortable, you can just stop and think and then read again. I think I want you to try that.

Owen: Okay.

Mrs. Bremwall works with two students on the same text in the same group. Cassie, she believes, has insufficient content knowledge to grasp the meaning of the passage. Mrs. Bremwall lets Cassie know that she believes this is the case, and then gives her the needed information. Because the point of this instructional interaction is not to learn about West Point, but instead, to learn about reading something that requires more knowledge than one might have, Mrs. Bremwall fills in the missing piece. The hope is that Cassie will remember this in future reading when she sees that a missing piece of knowledge hinders understanding. Of course, Mrs. Bremwall won't always be there for these moments, so she tries to model what Cassie might do on her own.

In the case of Owen, Mrs. Bremwall believes that activating prior knowledge about the subject will help meaning making. She coaches Owen to invoke what he knows as background for this piece of reading. Once she provides this coaching, she moves on to the next student.

In both cases, Mrs. Bremwall works on comprehension strategies with which the students are familiar. She has modeled the first strategy, doing further research, with her whole class numerous times. The second strategy, activating prior knowledge, has been used often in Owen's content-area studies.

Another area of instruction that teachers work on with students in strategic reading groups is vocabulary strategy use. We distinguish this kind of instruction—strategic vocabulary instruction—from other kinds of important work that teachers and students do around vocabulary. For instance, in whole group lessons, a teacher might introduce students to new vocabulary, especially around a particular concept under study. In a middle school class studying democracy, for instance, vocabulary around independence, declarations, manifest destiny, and the like might serve as classroom discussion. We call this *vocabulary study* and distinguish it from *vocabulary strategy instruction,* which is instruction in helping students find the meanings of unknown words they encounter in their reading.

Small group strategic reading instruction is the perfect place to see what students do and do not do when they come to an unfamiliar word, as the next example illustrates. Sebastian, an eighth grader, reads aloud from a printout of a website on extraterrestrial life (The search, n.d.):

Sebastian:	Most people have looked up at a starry sky and wondered whether there is life beyond our own blue planet. Is our world a unique oasis of life or are there other planets that harbor life? In the last 10 years advances in two areas of science have caused quite a stir with those interested in finding alien life. (para. 1)
Mrs. Mandell:	I hear that you stumbled over a word or two as you read. There are a lot of hard words in here, and I heard you read a couple of them in an unfamiliar tone. It made me think you might not understand them. Remember that sometimes it is just fine to read over troubling or unfamiliar words, especially if you can still understand the big concepts. Other times, it is not. For now, let's practice what we do when we come to an unknown word. This week, in my mini-lessons, I am going to work with the whole class on figuring out when you do need to stop and figure out words and when you do not. For now, let's assume these are needed words. The first one I heard you stumble on was this one. [points to *oasis*] How do you think you might go about determining what it means?
Sebastian:	Use the rest of the sentence?
Mrs. Mandell:	Okay, let's try it. Think through for me what you would do to use the rest of the sentence.
Sebastian:	I could see if the word is defined in the sentence? Or think about what sounds right in the sentence?
Mrs. Mandell:	Great. Those are really good strategies. What is your best guess based on what is there?

Sebastian: I really don't know . . . a place?

Mrs. Mandell: Of course you don't know; that is why you are guessing
                    and you made a good inference. You looked at the kind
                    of word it is and what would make sense and you got
                    awfully close. I want you to remember that strategy.

One interesting thing Mrs. Mandell does is not, in the end, give the word meaning to Sebastian. She understands that the point of the interaction is not to teach Sebastian what the word *oasis* means, but to have him think of some approaches to interrogating unknown words. The other thing to note is that Mrs. Mandell uses this interaction as her own data to plan instruction for the whole class. She knows that figuring out which words are and are not important in a text is a longer lesson than she can do in a 2-minute interaction, so she notes the need for follow-up and attends to something she really believes she can do in a short time. This looks so simple, but it is the kind of expert teaching we hope all students will encounter.

Cueing content-area texts. It is no secret that many of our middle school students struggle with reading content area textbooks. This can result in poor understanding of science or social studies or math that may have little to do with conceptual understandings of the content and everything to do with poor reading strategies.

Textbooks are a specialized genre of informational text that have particular importance for students of all grade levels. Strategic reading groups are a perfect site for helping students to understand effective ways to traverse content-area books. While all of the strategies used for informational text are also relevant to content-area textbooks, content textbooks are notoriously rich with text features (i.e., headings, preview questions, graphs, glossaries, bold or italicized words) that can really help a student with this difficult reading. Understanding how these features function will give students much more control over their reading and ultimately, more success.

We advise that teachers use older content-level texts or a chapter that is not currently under study when they work with these texts in strategic reading groups. Because our point is not to teach the content but to teach reading skills, using content that students are held accountable for can be a distraction and can confound strategic reading instruction. Once students have successful reading experiences with pieces of a textbook, they will gradually be able to generalize those experiences to the text portions that are assigned in their content-area course work.

Mr. Morton, as follows, is working with his students on reading from a biology text, Miller and Levine's (2010) *Biology*. The text is used in the ninth-grade high school classroom that many of these students will feed into the following year. This is a high-level group, so Mr. Morton selects this text to challenge them and allow them to practice the skills they will need the following year. He has arbitrarily chosen Chapter 24 on seed plants, and he has asked Jackson to read aloud before calling on Julia to do the same. The text asks two key questions in the left margin: (1) What adaptations allow seed plants to reproduce without open water? and (2) How does fertilization take place in gymnosperms in the absence of water? In addition, vocabulary that will be important in the text (*seed, gymnosperm, angiosperm, pollen grain, pollination, coat, ovule, pollen tube*) is highlighted, and the origin of the prefix *gymno* and the suffix *sperm* are provided.

Jackson: A characteristic shared by all seed plants is, as you might guess, the production of seeds. A seed is a plant embryo and a food supply encased in a protective covering. The living plant within a seed is diploid and represents the early developmental stage of the sporophyte phase of the plant life cycle.

Mr. Morton: I am going to have you stop there. Are you able to tell me what part of the plant life is indicated by the seed?

Jackson: It is before the plant?

Mr. Morton: It is. That is right. What in the text let you know that?

Jackson: I just knew it from before.

Mr. Morton: In a text like this with so much information, it is great to call on your background knowledge, but you don't want that to be the only thing that you do when you read. You want to use that background to help you to understand the text, not just rely on it entirely. If you knew everything already, would you need to read?

Jackson: No.

Mr. Morton: This time, I want you to go back and preview the information that comes even before the first paragraph because it will give you some definitions that will be helpful when you get to all this unfamiliar vocabulary. Really think about the definitions before starting and then, combined with your knowledge already, I bet you can come up with a really good understanding. Okay Julia, can you start reading aloud from where you are?

Julia: Nearly all gymnosperms bear their seeds directly on the scales of cones. In contrast, flowering plants or angiosperms, bear their seeds in flowers inside a layer of tissue that protects the seed.

Mr. Morton: I noticed you reading that really intently. Does it make sense?

Julia: Not really.

Mr. Morton: One thing this textbook does really well, and many textbooks do this, is support your understanding with illustrations. Do you see the graphic that shows the difference between gymnosperms and angiosperms? I know nothing about this either, but I bet that looking at that for a minute will help a lot because it looks like it isolates and categorizes the difference. Let's take a look at it. And I think, often, it is helpful to look at it even before you read as a way to prepare yourself for the content.

As these exchanges illustrate, Mr. Jackson himself lacks content knowledge about this topic. This is a unique opportunity, then, for him to help the students see how he might handle this kind of difficult reading. Textbooks have very common characteristics—including previews and supportive tables, pictures, and graphs—that students need to learn to look at carefully. Many students will benefit from doing this before they begin reading.

We think that content-area texts are ideal for use in strategic reading groups. Teacher and students benefit greatly from working together on these. At times, content-area teachers may want to pull a group and do similar instruction as that described in the previous example. Because they are expert in reading the texts that are available to students in their contents, they are able modelers. We encourage language arts teachers to invite content-area colleagues into their classrooms to observe the work they do in these groups and to discuss how they might use them in contexts other than language arts or reading.

6

Teacher Cueing During Narrative Text Reading

Many of the concepts related to cueing for informational text are also relevant to narrative fictional texts. Though we recommend that a large percentage of time spent in strategic reading groups focuses upon informational text, there is absolutely a place for cueing students as they read fiction.

EXAMPLES OF CUEING NARRATIVE TEXTS IN STRATEGIC READING GROUPS

Consider this example from eighth-grade teacher Ms. Martin working with a group on Shirley Jackson's (1948) short story "The Lottery." Ms. Martin has selected this text because it is brief, requires enormous inferencing skill, and will be a good challenge for the students. While it is a piece that Ms. Martin herself enjoys and appreciates, she believes that struggling through it will be a good use of this particular text for these particular students. After beginning the group, she circulates to the first of her four students:

Jonah: [reads aloud] The children assembled first, of course. School was recently over for the summer, and the feeling of liberty sat uneasily on most of them; they tended to gather together quietly for a while before they broke into boisterous play and their talk was still of the classroom and the teacher, of books and reprimands. (p. 1)

Ms. Martin: Okay, Jonah. I am going to have you stop there and look at me for a moment. What do you think was going through the children's minds as they assembled?

Jonah: Um, happy?

Ms. Martin: Happy, okay. Why?

Jonah: Because they had been waiting to … I think … I am not sure.

Ms. Martin: Okay, so we learned something here. We learned that we probably need to go back and figure out what is going on a little more clearly. I think one way to do this is to think about what the children were doing; really create almost like a movie in your head. See it, really see it.

Jonah: Should I do it now?

Ms. Martin: I am going on to the next student, but I want you to do it with this paragraph and then the next and the next. I will check back with you.

Ms. Martin works carefully with Jonah on an important comprehension strategy for fiction texts—creating a visual image. Her hope is that Jonah will practice this enough that it will become something he sometimes does automatically (which he likely already does with less challenging texts) and sometimes invokes explicitly when he is aware that he is not understanding. Recall from Chapter 4 the two-step process in helping students make meaning of difficult texts, a process that we call *cueing.* First, the teacher helps the students see that they don't have a handle on what is going on, or that what they understand is tentative and incomplete. Second, the teacher offers one thing that students can do to take control of a difficult reading.

Before we talk more explicitly about different kinds of cues, consider one more example from a sixth-grade class. The teacher, Mrs. Dunn, is working with the third of five students in the group on a fable from Hans Christian Andersen (1983). The fable, "The Bell-Deep," has simple language, but many of the turns of phrase are unfamiliar to even older children, and thus, it is a challenging read. Mrs. Dunn has already worked with the two previous students on some misunderstandings about the setting and context. She arrives as the third student, Monique, is reading from the second full paragraph, and now reads aloud for Mrs. Dunn:

Monique: In the Au grow the yellow water-lilies and brown feathery reeds; the dark velvety flag grows there, high and thick; old and decayed willows, slanting and tottering, hang far out over the stream beside the monk's meadow and by the bleaching ground; but opposite there are gardens upon gardens, each different from the rest, some with pretty flowers and bowers like little dolls' pleasure grounds, often displaying cabbage and other kitchen plants; and here and there the gardens cannot be seen at all, for the great elder trees that spread themselves out by the bank, and hang far out over the streaming waters, which are deeper here and there than an oar can fathom. Opposite the old nunnery is the deepest place, which is called the "bell-deep," and there dwells the old water spirit, the "Au-mann." (p. 588)

Mrs. Dunn: Okay, I am going to stop you there. Can you look at me and tell me what you think is the overriding characteristic of the setting that is being described?

Monique: It is a garden?

Mrs. Dunn: Well, yes, it is certainly a garden, but do you think we would need all that description just to say that this is set in a garden? There is a lot of stuff in here, and in narrative texts, stories like this, setting can create a mood or a tone that is very important to the development of the story. When I am reading along, I like to ask myself why they might be telling me so much about where it is. So I might do something like this: [reads aloud] . . . but opposite there are gardens upon gardens, each different from the rest, some with pretty flowers and bowers like little dolls' pleasure grounds …

    I wonder what they are trying to portray here? It must be something pleasant since they are talking about pretty flowers and dolls, so this is a pleasant scene so far. Okay, I think I am ready to read on and see if the rest of the description confirms or disconfirms this.

    Did you hear what I did? I asked myself a question about what all these details meant, I summarized what I thought they meant in my own head, and then I started to read on with that in mind. Do you think you could try that for the next little portion of this?

Mrs. Dunn also invokes the two-step process whereby she tries to get Monique to see the limits of her answer, and then offers a strategy so that Monique might know one thing to do when she confronts a description like this in the future. This process looks simple, but it takes some understandings. Some of those understandings were discussed in the previous chapter on cueing informational text reading.

Recall that there are roughly two kinds of meaning-making break-downs. In the first, students are confronted with text in which they either struggle or actively elect not to attend. A simple reread can sometimes solve these attending breakdowns. Other times, they require a reread and an explicit strategy. In the second type of meaning-making breakdown, the student may be very actively attending, yet the meaning making is hindered by understanding—by unfamiliar vocabulary, lack of content knowledge, or deficiency in conceptual understandings required to process the text. In this second case, often, different kinds of strategies are necessary and it won't often help to merely reread. It may be helpful to refer back to Chapter 5 for a more complete discussion of these two kinds of meaning-making breakdowns.

DETERMINING WHEN MEANING HAS BROKEN DOWN IN NARRATIVE TEXTS

Teachers select narrative texts for small group strategic reading instruction because they expect the students to struggle with the texts. In Chapter 4, we listed the four Ps—common things to listen for when students read aloud. Upon hearing these things (i.e., slow or quick **p**ace, uneven **p**rosody, reading through **p**unctuation, and **p**ushing through miscues), teachers often are correct in assuming that students are struggling to make meaning. Sometimes, however, teachers hear nothing to indicate that students are not making meaning of text, yet they wonder. The kinds of questions teachers ask students when working with narrative texts are often slightly different from the questions they ask when working with informational texts. For instance, it would be inappropriate to ask students to summarize a narrative text the way we might ask them to summarize a piece of informational text. Similarly, we likely wouldn't ask them to "tell me what you just learned." Instead, we adjust our questions to the particular demands of a narrative text. Table 6.1 lists some of these questions.

As we discussed in the previous chapter on informational text, we urge teachers to expect much from an answer to their questions about the

Table 6.1   Questions to Ask to Determine Understanding of Narrative Text

What just happened?

What do you predict will happen next?

Can you retell this passage?

What do you think is motivating this character?

What do we know about the setting?

Can you compare this character to another?

reading. Almost any reader can fake an answer, as shown in the following example from a seventh-grade strategic reading group working on an excerpt from Jules Verne's (1870) *Twenty Thousand Leagues Under the Sea.* Jaden has finished reading a paragraph from the first chapter. Ms. Lawson stops him:

Ms. Lawson: What do you predict will happen with this monster?

Jaden: He will sink ships?

Ms. Lawson: What in the text makes you say that?

Jaden: I'm not sure.

Ms. Lawson: It is absolutely fine not to be sure, but we want to make predictions that are based on things we have read. A good strategy for reading stories is to think about what will happen next, but we have to know what happened, really solidly, in order to think about the next thing. What could you do to have a fuller understanding of the events surrounding the monster so that you might make a text-based prediction?

Jaden gathered enough of the text to know that there was talk of a monster and talk of peril at sea, yet he missed much of the subtlety surrounding the story. We want to show students how to test themselves about what they are understanding and hold themselves to very high standards of meaning making as they read text that challenges them. Ms. Lawson understood that the meaning Jaden was making was tentative and incomplete, so she asked him a question that might illuminate these loose understandings for both of them. Then, she reminded him to be very specific in his understandings of difficult text, otherwise he would read through them without thinking hard enough about them to make sense.

Many teachers have one or two go-to questions. They ask the same kind of question of many different kinds of stories, such as those seen in Table 6.1. This helps keep the teachers focused on the task at hand and helps prepare the students, as time goes by, to ready themselves for the question—a strategy in and of itself, or to ask themselves the same questions as they read. Sometimes students reply to our questions by saying "I don't know" or something in that vein, but more often they seem to think they do know something that is just a piece of an understanding. These questions are designed to help them see what they don't know.

As with informational texts, there are certainly times when students do understand, sufficiently, what they have just read. This may be because the text was not as hard as we thought; it may be because students are demonstrating the use of strategies they may not have used previously; it may be because of the particular features of a given text. For whatever reason, we don't go looking for problems just so that we can feel successful in our instruction. Instead, we ask students to explain how they made meaning as they read, in order to reinforce the strategy they used, as illustrated in the next example. Teo has just read from a difficult short story, and Mr. Bright is questioning him to find out what he is able to understand from the story:

Mr. Bright: You read that beautifully. What do you think is motivating the character to treat another person that way?

Teo: I think she is feeling really insecure about herself, so instead of feeling that hurt she is trying to hurt someone else.

Mr. Bright: And what in the text that you just read made you think that?

Teo: She said that she felt herself turning her hate outward. So to me that meant directed to another person.

Mr. Bright: I think that is a really good analysis. I like how you paid so much attention to how she might have been feeling and then made that inference. I hope you will continue to use that strategy as you read. Well done.

Mr. Bright wanted Teo to consider the strategies he'd used to make sense of his reading. In asking Teo to explain his thinking, Mr. Bright drew attention to it, allowing Teo to become metacognitive, aware of his own thinking processes, a characteristic of particularly strong readers.

STRATEGIES TO PRACTICE WITH NARRATIVE TEXTS

Once teachers believe that students are not in full control of their understanding, they prepare to cue students with a strategy they believe might help in the future. Because attending cues are often handled differently than meaning cues, we discuss them separately in reference to narrative texts the way we did with informational texts in the previous chapter. Attending cues and meaning cues for narrative texts are listed in Table 6.2. As we mentioned in Chapter 5, sometimes these cues do overlap.

When students' meaning breakdowns are largely due to lack of attention, we give them strategies to help them pay attention. As teachers well know, understanding and reading stories that one does not choose is part of a student's academic life. Students may not understand a story not because it is too difficult, but because they are not invested in it and do not care about its meaning or outcomes. This should be acknowledged as a fact of life; nobody is interested in everything. Yet, students must work to

Table 6.2   Attending and Meaning Cues for Narrative Texts

Attending Cues	Genre
Go back and reread.	Use vocabulary strategies to get at meanings of unknown words.
Go back and reread in smaller chunks.	Connect to prior knowledge.
Annotate the text—highlight, underline, make notations.	Talk with someone who is reading or has read the book.
Connect the story or character to self, world, or other text.	Do research on the setting, plot elements, genre, or time period.
Imagine what the scene, character, or events look like.	Use knowledge of narrative structure or literary tropes.

understand how to engage even when it is not of their own choosing. The attending cues listed in Table 6.2 are similar to those found in the chapter on informational texts, yet are specific to story.

In the next example, Mrs. Dreyer works with her eighth graders on the short story "The Bridge" by Lorin Cranford (1996). Notice how she works with Jason and Connor differently, given that she recognizes one student as struggling with an attending difficulty, and the next student with a meaning difficulty:

Mrs. Dreyer: Jason, as you were reading, I noticed that you read right through the punctuation—that made me think you were struggling to assign meaning to the words and were just sort of reading without thinking. Can you go back and think about your reading, as you read? Don't move on until you understand that you are listening to yourself carefully. Can you do that? I would bet that you can't retell that passage, right? It is fine; let's see what happens on another reading.

Okay, Connor, let me hear you read aloud wherever you are in your reading.

Connor: [reads aloud] Anything's better'n here. Nothin' but hard concrete. Those walls—cold, mean, just like a prison! I remember that time in Pecos. There, we had four walls and a roof over our head. Boy, did we make the money! That cotton was really thick. In one day, I raked in 25 bucks! By Saturday night I was ready to live it up. All slicked up we hit town to party! Things was a goin' all right til Jack got drunk. Then he wanted to fight. He would have to pick on the sheriff's son. Boy, did that bust up the dance! Man, it broke our pocket books too! Should have left him in jail.

That rat! He's been the cause of many fast get-aways from town. Just ain't never learned to leave fightin' alone. Guess he's got to have some excitement, though. Sure ain't none in a cotton patch! (p. 1)

Mrs. Dreyer: What do we know about the time and place you are reading about?

Connor: Um, the past?

Mrs. Dreyer: How do you know and can you be more concrete? Are there clues about when in the past or where?

Connor: I don't know.

Mrs. Dreyer: It is hard to figure it out, I agree. I think we want to look very carefully at the dialect and all the references to cotton. What might those things tell us?

Connor: Not sure.

Mrs. Dreyer: Well, I think it is going to be hard to continue without knowing. I am going to ask you to do this, can you please read another two paragraphs and see if you can find any clues to the time or the place, anything else you notice in the dialect. Does this dialect remind you of any other things we have read? I think that will help. So you know what to do?

Connor: See if I can read a little more and get some more clues about where and when it is?

Mrs. Dreyer: Yes, great.

These students have very different needs even on the same brief text. Jason, the teacher believes, has difficulty because he is not assigning meaning to the words he recites. Instead of reading, he is word calling. This is a perfectly decodable text and he has no trouble saying the words, but Mrs. Dreyer hears something in the reading—Jason is not stopping at appropriate places in the text—which leads her to believe that meaning isn't being made. She believes, based on what she knows of Jason, that drawing explicit attention to this will be enough to draw him back into meaning making. Connor seems to be attending as best as he can, yet he lacks background knowledge about dialect and historic references (i.e., cotton picking) to sufficiently infer time and place. Having Connor reread will not be effective, so Mrs. Dreyer offers a strategy that might. Neither Jason nor Connor has made sufficient meaning of this text, yet the strategies Mrs. Dreyer offers are customized for their individual and unique needs. This is the particular contribution of this kind of customized instruction. A teacher could not do this kind of teaching in a large group or by hearing only one student read aloud. The structure of strategic reading groups is set up in such a way that this intense and individualized instructional work is possible.

7

Materials for Strategic Reading Groups

Finding materials to meet the needs of all students in a class is a common concern of middle grade teachers. Many middle schools lack the leveled texts that are more commonly found in elementary schools, so middle school teachers are often at a loss to find texts that are appropriate for their below and above grade-level students.

Though more and more middle schools are beginning to accumulate leveled texts, and more and more textbook publishers are including leveled texts with their basal readers, we believe it is possible to address students' needs without purchasing loads of new leveled materials. This chapter looks at a variety of different materials that teachers can use for strategic reading groups. First, however, we consider the most important points to remember when choosing materials for strategic reading groups.

CHOOSING MATERIALS

Materials must present a challenge.

Teachers want their students to be successful. It feels good to listen to students read fluently, and to know that they are not struggling to comprehend. However, it is important to remember that in strategic reading, we *want* students to make mistakes when they read because when they do, we have the opportunity to (1) learn something about what our students do when they are faced with a reading difficulty, and (2) provide on-the-spot instruction that will help them get through that difficulty.

When students learn that they can use strategies to overcome the difficulties they have with reading, they feel successful. When they are not asked to read materials that pose challenges for them, they do not get this same sense of success.

Consider the following two interactions between Mr. Matthews and his fifth-grade student, Bethany. The first shows a strategic reading interaction when the text is too easy, and the second shows an interaction when the text provides a sufficient challenge.

Scenario 1

Mr. Matthews is listening to Bethany read a Level Q text entitled *Cut Down to Size at High Noon: A Math Adventure* (Sundby, 2000). Bethany doesn't make any decoding errors, though she does read the name Louie as "Lou," a miscue that doesn't concern Mr. Matthews. She reads slowly, but with good expression. After about a minute of listening to her read, Mr. Matthews covers up the text and asks, "Can you tell me in your own words what you just read?" Bethany provides a detailed retelling, and Mr. Matthews is satisfied that she understood the passage. "Great job reading today, Bethany!" he says, and he moves on to the next student.

Scenario 2

Mr. Matthews is listening to Bethany read a Level S text entitled *Cuts, Scrapes, Scabs, and Scars* (Silverstein, Silverstein, & Nunn, 1999). Bethany reads more haltingly than when she read the previous text, and when she gets to the sentence, "The epidermis is about as thick as a piece of paper—much thinner than the keratin layer" (p. 10), she clearly decodes the word *epidermis* syllable by syllable. Here is the interaction that follows:

Mr. Matthews: I'm going to stop you there. I heard you really slow down when you said *epidermis*. You pronounced it correctly, but I'm wondering if you know what it is.

Bethany: No, I really don't. I know it has to do with skin, but I'm not sure how.

Mr. Matthews: You're right; it does have to do with skin. Let's look back at this page. Do you notice something that might help you figure out exactly what the epidermis is?

Bethany: [notices a diagram of a cross-section of skin and points it out to Mr. Matthews]

Mr. Matthews: Yes … why don't you read the caption and see if that helps you.

Bethany: [reads caption to herself] Oh, I get it! The epidermis is this pink layer of the skin. [points] It's underneath the keratin and it's living skin.

Mr. Matthews: Great job. You came to a word you didn't understand, but you used the diagram to help you make sense of it. When you're reading later in social studies, I want you to remember this strategy. Often when you're reading informational text, you'll come to new and challenging words, but if you remember to use text features like diagrams, you'll often find that you can figure out the words.

During the first scenario, Bethany read fluently and was able to understand the passage. This is exactly the kind of experience we'd want students to have when they are reading by themselves, with no one around to guide them. However, during strategic reading, the teacher spends precious time listening to students read in order to provide on-the-spot instruction tailored specifically to individual students. If there are no breakdowns in decoding, vocabulary, or comprehension, then it is really wasted time. Rather than helping Bethany get over a difficult spot, Mr. Matthews is only able to compliment her and move on. It seems obvious to us that this is not a productive use of one-on-one instructional time, but we often observe teachers who are afraid to use challenging texts, because they do not like to see their students struggle.

A question that comes up over and over when we work with teachers is, "Doesn't using difficult texts make students feel bad about themselves as readers?" Or, "Aren't students embarrassed to read when they struggle to read words or make meaning?" The truth is, students will not become appreciably better readers if they don't get practice reading something difficult for them. If they never face difficult texts, they will never know what to do when it does happen, and for nearly all of us, it will. It may not be until college, but many of us have experienced being in a challenging course and having few strategies with which to help us understand the course materials. We do our students no favors by never giving them texts that make them struggle, because we want them to know what to do if they are faced with challenging material. In addition, we find that student confidence actually increases when they see that they do have strategies for reading and understanding difficult texts. It feels good to face challenges head-on and overcome them.

Below-level readers, too, need this kind of challenge. Often teachers don't trust their struggling readers to be able to overcome adversity when they read. They mistakenly believe that reading easy texts during small group instruction will build student confidence. The truth is, though, that our struggling readers need confidence that they can figure out complex texts on their own, and they don't get this unless they struggle *with our support.* Consider how often struggling students face difficult texts (without teacher support) during the day: during science and social studies class, where texts are generally at or slightly above grade level; in language arts, where they must often attempt to read the same novel the rest of the class is reading; in math class, where solving story problems depends on being able to analyze what they read. They continually confront materials that are too hard for them, yet teachers seem reluctant to pull texts for small group instruction that are as hard as what they encounter throughout their reading day.

Some thoughts on book levels. We owe much to Marie Clay's (2006) concept of independent-, instructional-, and frustration-level texts. Her work has allowed us to consider how students should read different kinds of texts at different times and for different instructional purposes. Recall from concepts introduced earlier, independent-level texts are those that students can read on their own, decoding with 96 to 100 percent accuracy. Instructional-level texts, those that students can decode with 90 to 95 percent accuracy, are seen as the ideal match for traditional guided reading instruction, because students are challenged, but not to the point of frustration. Frustration-level texts are those that students decode with less than 90 percent accuracy. These levels work pretty well in primary grades, when decoding is one of the instructional foci, and in our work with primary teachers we advise that they choose texts at the *high instructional* level for guided reading (meaning texts that students can decode with about 90 percent accuracy); however, these levels become less meaningful for students in middle school.

The problem for most of our middle school students is not that they have trouble decoding, but that they are have trouble understanding what they read. Often middle school students will read with 100 percent accuracy, yet still fail to provide an accurate retelling or identify the main idea. We have seen teachers who keep moving students through levels because of their accuracy, and never ask or expect students to answer questions about what they've read beyond the most superficial measures of comprehension. In addition, we have read compelling research (e.g., Boyle, 2011) indicating that leveling systems are not especially accurate when it comes to informational texts. While students may be able to decode a Level S informational text as easily as a Level S fiction text, the demands of informational text (including text features such as diagrams, text boxes, captions, etc.) can make comprehension of that text more challenging than the fiction text.

We are concerned about the emphasis being placed on book levels in light of this problem. Certainly comprehension is built into many assessment systems (where being able to answer comprehension questions with about 75 percent accuracy is considered instructional), but it is not built into all, and in many school buildings, fluency measures are the primary assessment tool for determining student reading level, very often without any attention to comprehension.

Instead of being beholden to book levels, teachers should concentrate on finding books or other reading materials that they know will provide a significant challenge for students, regardless of the level, or even if the materials are not leveled at all. While we agree that the idea of book leveling has helped teachers to consider each of their student's instructional needs, we also believe that schools are awash with leveling mania, and we know that teachers are very hesitant to put students into groups until they have student levels all figured out.

Keep it brief.

We sometimes encounter middle school teachers who want to use novels for their strategic reading instruction. We discourage this for two reasons: First of all, strategic guided reading is hard and deliberate work. As we said previously, teachers should be choosing books that are too difficult for students to read on their own. Often during a strategic reading group, students have trouble reading the material independently, and they wait until the teacher comes to listen to them read. They generally can't read more than a few pages during the group time. Because they may only read the book about two times per week, novel reading becomes a slow and frustrating process, taking several weeks or months to complete the book. Students don't have time in this setting to discuss and become engaged with a story. It is our philosophy that strategic reading isn't a time to delve into a really great book; it's a time for students to practice using strategies to help them when they face challenges.

The second reason we discourage using novels for strategic reading instruction is because we believe that the materials teachers use should be brief—something students can finish in one or two strategic reading sessions, such as short stories, chapters from an old content-area textbook, newspaper or magazine articles, the short booklets that come with basal readers, and so on. Teachers also can use pieces of longer texts without feeling obligated to complete them. In this way, teachers expose students to many different genres and the text features that go with each, and also avoid the frustration that comes with reading something in small bits, over an extended period of time.

Consider subject matter.

Many teachers we know feel strongly about making strategic materials relevant to other areas of their literacy (or content-area) instruction. For example, if students are studying World War II in social studies, teachers try to find strategic reading materials that have to do with World War II.

As it is already hard enough trying to find materials that best meet the needs of all of our students, to try to find materials that correspond with other areas of the curriculum is unnecessary. It is important to remember that materials used in strategic reading instruction are for practice. Students practice strategies with challenging texts that we then hope they will transfer to texts they read on their own, at home, or at school. Our goal in choosing materials for strategic reading is to find texts that will reinforce helpful reading strategies, not to reinforce content students may be learning in other classes. If we choose a book on black holes to read with a group of students, it is not our goal that students will learn all about black holes. Rather, in each of our interactions with the students in the group, our goal is that students will practice using a strategy that will help them no matter what they are reading. As such, it may be that one of our strategic groups will read about Jacques Cousteau while another will read about desert animals, while still another may read about the women's suffrage movement.

Because we do not expect students to master the content of the material they read in strategic reading groups, we cannot hold them accountable for that material. We would never quiz students on the content, nor would we send students back to their desks to do any kind of follow-up work. Because we've chosen the book primarily because it's a significant challenge for students, to expect them to do any kind of independent work with it would be unfair. We may sometimes decide not to even finish a book or article.

Informational texts. One recommendation we do have about subject matter is to focus as much as possible on informational text. Research is clear about the fact that American students tend to be weak in informational text reading (e.g., Daniels, 1990; Duke & Pearson, 2002). Our readers may be aware of a phenomenon called the *fourth-grade slump*, which is when students who have been doing fine in reading through third grade begin to struggle with reading. Many have attributed this to the fact that students are expected to read and understand more and more content-area texts as they move into intermediate and middle grades (e.g., Chall, Jacobs, & Baldwin, 1990). We believe that strategic reading groups are an ideal setting to provide students with the teacher support they so clearly need. This support aims to reinforce the comprehension and vocabulary strategies that will help them successfully negotiate informational texts within and outside of school, in print and online form.

To summarize, the materials we choose for strategic reading should be challenging enough that students demonstrate a breakdown in meaning, encounter an unknown vocabulary word, or have trouble decoding relatively quickly, generally within the first minute of their reading. Materials should not be too long and should never be the kind of "great" literature that would be best read aloud, or read during literature study. Finally, teachers should save their energy for the tough work of prompting students during strategic reading, and not spend it on finding books that are thematically connected to the curriculum.

As a reminder, if teachers do choose books that are either too easy or way too challenging for their group, they should remember how easy it is to fix that situation, by choosing books that are harder or easier the next time they meet with the group. It will not damage students to have one strategic reading group where the materials do not meet their needs, as long as the teacher recognizes this and changes the material difficulty the next time she meets with the group.

FINDING APPROPRIATE MATERIALS

There are many potential sources of reading materials that are appropriate for middle-level strategic reading. Textbook publishers now do much more for middle grades with regards to leveled texts, but even without such texts, there are plenty of options. This section looks at all the different materials middle school teachers can consider for their strategic reading groups.

Publisher Leveled Books

Textbook publishers have certainly jumped on the leveled text bandwagon and schools now often buy, with their new textbook purchases, bundles of texts for use during small group reading instruction. Even social studies and science textbooks now often come with these types of leveled texts. If a school has purchased texts like these, they are certainly a great resource to have. One issue that teachers have is that these texts often only come in three basic levels: below grade level, at grade level, and above grade level. As teachers well know, it is a rare class indeed where students fall neatly into three levels like this, and when teachers try to divide their students into three groups in order to be able to use these leveled books, they find that some students are not appropriately challenged, because they are either significantly above or below grade level.

If a school has leveled texts like these, we recommend that teachers across grade levels pool their resources, so that a sixth-grade teacher looking for a more challenging text can use one from an eighth-grade teacher, and that eighth-grade teacher can go to her colleagues in lower grades to find an appropriate text for her lowest group.

While we are happy to see publishers address the issue of differentiation, we are concerned about the additional materials that come with leveled texts. The accompanying teacher guides are often scripted, and if teachers follow the script, they end up running groups that focus on a particular strategy rather than letting students demonstrate, through their own reading, what they need on any given day. There are also lots of supplementary materials for students to use during and after reading, including graphic organizers, and other worksheets designed to be completed after leaving the group. As mentioned previously, students should not be sent back to their desks to complete tasks related to their strategic reading book, because, if chosen properly, it will be too difficult for them to work with independently. We would much rather see students reading materials they've chosen or writing about topics that interest them when they work independently, instead of struggling to complete worksheets. We advise teachers to certainly make use of the leveled texts that come with their reading and other content area texts, but not necessarily to use the supplementary materials that accompany them.

Magazine or Newspaper Articles

Many teachers subscribe to magazines or bring newspapers into class for their students to read. These can make great texts for strategic reading groups. Refer to Table 7.1 for a list of journals that are appropriate for middle-level readers of all ability levels. *Weekly Reader,* a staple in many elementary classrooms, has a series of middle grade journals such

Table 7.1   Print Magazines and Newspapers for Middle-Level Readers

Below-Level Readers	*Scholastic Action* (middle and secondary grade–appropriate content written at a third- to fifth-grade level) *Time for Kids* *Sports Illustrated for Kids* *National Geographic for Kids*
At-Level Readers	*Weekly Reader* Journals: • *Current Events* • *Current Health Kids* • *Current Science* Scholastic Journals: • *Junior Scholastic* (social studies content) • *Scholastic Scope* (language arts content) • *Scholastic Math* • *Science World* Periodicals written for adults (e.g., *Time, Sports Illustrated, U.S. News and World Report*)
Above-Level Readers	*The New York Times* *The Economist* *Science* *National Geographic*

as *Current Events, Current Health Kids,* and *Current Science* that are ideally suited to strategic reading work. With articles short enough to read over one or two days, lots of nonfiction text features to reinforce, and topics of interest to our students, these kinds of materials can be appropriate for students across different instructional levels.

Another classroom standby, *Scholastic News,* also has journals for middle grade students. *Junior Scholastic* (with middle grade social studies content), *Scholastic Scope* (with language arts related content), *Scholastic Math,* and *Science World* all contain articles perfect for use during strategic reading. The Scholastic journal *Scholastic Action* has content appropriate for middle school and high school students but is written at a third- to fifth-grade level, making it perfect for strategic reading with the most struggling readers.

Many magazines have editions specifically for students, including *National Geographic, Time, Sports Illustrated,* and so on. Because these magazines provide material at different reading levels, they can be quite appropriate for our students who read below grade level. For at- and above-level readers, we can use the regular version of these magazines, which tend to be written at about a seventh- or eighth-grade reading level. We have had great success using newspaper articles, including op-ed pieces from the *New York Times,* for our highest achieving students whose reading capabilities far exceed even the Level Z reading materials publishers provide.

Textbooks

Often when schools purchase a new language arts, science, or social studies textbook, the old textbook is discarded or donated, or consigned to a dusty life on a hard-to-reach shelf. Though we certainly don't want our students reading outdated or disproven material (e.g., geography that includes information about the USSR or science texts that still refer to Pluto as a planet), often schools replace texts that are still relatively current. These texts can be ideal for strategic reading, because we can target our strategic reading work to helping students navigate textbooks, typically the most challenging kind of reading our students do. We can also access materials at different grade levels, so that seventh-grade teachers can use old fifth- or sixth-grade textbooks for their below-level readers, while using eighth- or ninth-grade textbooks for their above-level readers. Retired textbooks can provide reading material for a whole year's worth of strategic reading, if necessary (though we do recommend varying the materials used during strategic reading to retain student interest and expose them to a variety of genres).

Short Stories or Literature Anthologies

While we don't recommend using novels, because of the length of time they would take to complete during a strategic reading setting, and because strategic reading isn't ideally suited for the kinds of grand conversations teachers and students like to have about novels, short stories can work quite nicely during strategic reading. Just as we often have old textbooks gathering dust on our shelves, we also have old literature anthologies lying around. The nice thing about these anthologies is that they don't become outdated in the same way content-area texts may, and we can often find stories that are well suited, in length and difficulty, for our strategic reading groups.

It is ideal if a dedicated space can be made available for strategic reading materials, such that all grade-level teachers within a school can store their materials together, to make it easier for each teacher to find materials appropriate for all of their students. There is no reason for the seventh-grade language arts teachers to house all the seventh-grade level materials in their rooms, when sixth- and eighth-grade teachers also have students reading at the seventh-grade level.

Online Sources

In addition to print materials, teachers now have access to ample online materials. News outlets such as CNN provide materials appropriate for students, and many of our students can read adult-level materials as well. In addition to subscribing to print materials, schools can also use online newspapers and magazines, often for free. Table 7.2 lists some online sites suitable for printing out middle grade–appropriate texts.

Table 7.2   Online Sources of Strategic Reading Material

www.headlinespot.com/for/kids	This site provides links to online material appropriate for kids, on topics such as current events, science, the environment, and sports.
www.cnn.com/studentnews/	This site provides a 10-minute news video each day on a current events topic. The transcripts provided for each show are useful for strategic reading and can be printed out and read during group work.
www.newscurrents.com	This site is accessible only by subscription but provides access to *Read to Know*, an online news magazine for Grades 6 and up. It also provides access to NewsCurrents, an interactive current events discussion program.

(continued)

Table 7.2   (continued)

http://learning.blogs.nytimes.com/	Teachers can print out articles from the regular *New York Times* site (www .nytimes.com), but this site, titled The Learning Network, provides additional materials for students, including access to blog posts appropriate for our students as well as teacher resources.

In short, we want students and teachers to start work with strategic reading groups without undue stress about gathering materials. It is also worth noting that the first year that teachers undertake strategic reading groups is often the most time intensive, with regard to finding appropriate materials. This initial investment of time pays off in subsequent years, because the materials gathered during the first year can be used in subsequent years.

8

Assessment Prior to and During Strategic Reading Groups

One of the things that teachers often say to us is how challenging it is to accurately assess students prior to beginning small group reading instruction. Teachers are concerned about getting assessment "just right." They worry that they will place students in the wrong group, or that a child who reads very fluently will have comprehension issues that they won't be able to catch. We are sympathetic to these concerns, but we honestly believe that teachers need to relax a bit when it comes to determining the just-right reading group for their students.

One of the great things about strategic reading groups is the level of flexibility teachers have in re-forming groups. Unlike the way reading groups have worked historically in education, strategic reading groups are not set in stone. We know that in the 1970s and 1980s, for example, when children were placed in reading groups in first grade, they were often tracked for years, so that if they were in the struggling reading group at age 6, they were likely still in the struggling reading group at age 12. We like to think that this has changed dramatically. Nowadays, if a teacher places a child in a group and he either reads and understands flawlessly or he struggles to the point that he can't even begin to understand what he's read, the teacher can easily move him to another group.

Strategic reading groups are fluid and easily changeable. Teachers can assess whether or not students are placed appropriately just by listening as they read.

This chapter covers assessment of students prior to beginning strategic reading groups, and also looks at how strategic reading groups themselves act as an on-the-spot assessment of students' strengths and weaknesses. It also gives significant data on the appropriateness of their placement.

ASSESSING PRIOR TO BEGINNING STRATEGIC READING

From the moment students enter our classrooms, we begin to assess them. We notice the kinds of books or reading materials they are drawn to, the ease with which they can or cannot engage with a text, their oral reading ability, their interest in the stories or novels we read aloud, their willingness to write about or discuss what they've read. All of the information we gather about our students at the beginning of the school year, even before we begin doing formal or informal reading assessments, is data that can help us begin to understand our students' reading strengths and needs. We often tell teachers that we believe they could probably divide students into groups after knowing their students for about a week, and be relatively successful in doing so, even without the data they gain from diagnostic reading assessments (e.g., fluency measures, Measures of Academic Progress, informal reading inventories, etc.).

It is true, however, that sometimes our students surprise us. There is always a student who reads aloud very haltingly or who hesitates to become engaged in class discussions, yet turns out to have a great vocabulary, important background knowledge, and much better than expected comprehension. Conversely, there are also students who read aloud beautifully, with great expression, and who present themselves as strong students, yet nonetheless have difficulties when asked to retell a story or answer comprehension questions. For this reason, we think it is important to assess students prior to placing them in reading groups. The following are some ideas about ways to assess middle school students.

Reading Conferences

During the first weeks of school, as teachers prepare students to work independently in anticipation of small group strategic reading (see Chapter 9 for more on this topic), students will likely spend time each day reading self-selected texts. While they do this, we recommend that teachers walk around the room, or call students to their desk, to ask them about what they have chosen to read and to hear them read a bit out loud. In so doing, the teacher attains a sense of the kinds of reading materials that interest the students, the difficulty of those reading materials, and the students' ability to read fluently and understand what they read. Such conferences should take no more than 5 minutes, and as such, the teacher can meet with two or three students during independent reading time each day and can easily meet with all of her students within two to three weeks. Such a conference might look like the following exchange Mrs. Bedford had with one of her seventh graders:

Mrs. Bedford: So, what are you reading today, Peter?

Peter: *On the Court With . . . LeBron James* by Matt Christopher (2008).

Mrs. Bedford: Oh, okay. Why did you choose this book?

Peter: Well, I'm on the basketball team, and I am just really interested in basketball. Also, I think LeBron James is a really great athlete.

Mrs. Bedford: Those are all good reasons to read this book! So will you please read a bit for me, right where you left off?

Peter: [reads a couple pages aloud]

While Peter reads, Mrs. Bedford notices that he reads slowly, without much expression in his voice. Yet he doesn't stumble over many words, and he seems quite engaged.

Mrs. Bedford: Great reading, Peter. Can you tell me about what you just read?

Peter: Yeah, well, after LeBron's family had to move out of LeBron's grandma's house, they couldn't all stay together anymore. LeBron and his mom moved into a bad neighborhood where there was lots of violence. They didn't have their own place. They stayed with friends of his mom.

Mrs. Bedford: A lot of bad things have happened so far in LeBron's life. I sure hope things get better for LeBron. Will you let me know?

After Peter goes back to his desk, Mrs. Bedford jots some things down in her anecdotal record notebook. Table 8.1 provides an illustration of what these anecdotal notes might look like.

In just a couple minutes, Mrs. Bedford has learned a lot about Peter and his reading.

She knows that his independent reading book is about two years below grade level, that he is interested in reading about sports, that his fluency

Table 8.1   Mrs. Bedford's Anecdotal Notes From Reading Conference

Student name: Peter F.

Name of book: *On the Court With . . . LeBron James* by Matt Christopher

Too hard/too easy/just right: I think just right. Peter understands the storyline; reads slowly, but shows good comprehension; very engaged in story.

Book level: Not sure—definitely below seventh-grade level, probably fifth grade? I need to check on this.

Comments: Peter likes to read about sports, especially basketball. Would like to see what he does with a book at a similar level if it's not on a topic he knows a lot about. Keep an eye on fluency.

isn't great but his comprehension is fine, at least with this high-interest book. The next time Mrs. Bedford conferences with Peter, she may well ask him to read a slightly more challenging book to see what he does when he encounters unknown words, and to ascertain how he comprehends when he reads more difficult material.

Conducting brief conferences like this provides teachers with evidence about their students' reading that can inform their decisions about student placement in strategic reading groups, as well as the strengths and challenges of each of their students. We recommend conferencing on an ongoing basis.

Fluency Measures

The information provided by fluency measures is limited. Even so, these measures are often a required assessment in schools and thus available as a partial window into student reading. Because fluency measures are supposed to be administered using grade-level passages, teachers can quickly see which students are likely reading below, at, and above grade level. For example, if a sixth-grade teacher uses the same sixth-grade-level passage for all of her students, she can easily see which students have especially high rate and accuracy, who has good accuracy but reads slowly, who reads quickly but with lower accuracy, and who reads slowly and struggles to decode. This information alone can help the teacher begin to think about how her students may fall into groups. However, one thing that is missing from this information is anything to do with comprehension. For this reason, we believe the best use of fluency measures is as a rough estimation that a comprehension assessment then confirms or disconfirms.

One way to do this is to inform students prior to reading that they are going to be asked some comprehension questions about what they read. Though a comprehension check can be part of fluency measures, it is our experience that students are rarely asked to summarize or retell fluency passages. Students have come to think of fluency passages as something to be read as quickly as possible, so it is only fair to give them a heads up if we're going to check their understanding as well. We usually administer fluency measures according to protocol, timing students for 1 minute, counting the number of words read in that time, subtracting words skipped or read incorrectly, and coming up with a WCPM (words correct per minute). Often students do not finish the passage during the minute, so when we go on to do a comprehension check, we will say, "Now I'd like you to read this whole passage silently to yourself. Start at the beginning and read carefully, because I'm going to ask you to retell the passage in your own words when you're done reading."

This practice allows students to see that understanding the passage, not reading quickly, is the goal of this portion of the assessment. When they complete the assessment, the teacher can ask a student to do a retelling, without looking back at the passage. The teacher jots down notes while the student does this, observing whether or not the student understands the main idea of the passage, the level of details provided, and so forth. If the retelling is brief or incomplete, the teacher can ask some pointed questions about the passage. Sometimes students cannot remember everything themselves, but with prompting from the teacher, via questions, they can remember additional details. Taking notes as the student answers questions, the teacher records whether or not the student got the gist of the story, whether she could provide supporting details, or if her recall of details was random and not germane to the main idea.

When teachers take some additional time to check comprehension during administration of fluency measures, they glean much richer information about their students' reading than simply how fast or how accurately they read. They learn, too, if the students understand what they read. This information is particularly interesting when a teacher discovers that he has a student who reads aloud accurately and quickly, but with little comprehension, or when he discovers that a student he thought was a struggling reader because of disjointed or labored oral reading actually comprehends material quite well.

Informal Reading Inventories

There are many kinds of informal reading inventories (IRIs) produced by publishers and educational institutions. IRIs are lengthy and detailed and most often administered outside the classroom by reading specialists or literacy interventionists. The results of these can be helpful as they identify student level as well as their strengths and weaknesses.

Most IRIs incorporate running records. These are fantastic ways to understand how beginning readers decode and recognize sight words. For fluent readers, running records are of limited benefit. Even in the middle grades, using running records with the most struggling readers may be beneficial. Clay (2000) and Shea (2006) provide more information about running records and how they can inform a teacher's assessment of middle grade students.

Formal Assessment Data

One thing that is not missing from our students' records is assessment reports. Though we don't ever want to base our understanding of students exclusively on scores from standardized tests or other previous years' assessment data, we certainly can see how our students performed on assessments and begin to use that data to consider potential group placement. Typically, standardized tests report scaled scores for each student. Based on that score, student work falls into one of four categories: (1) exceeds standards, (2) meets standards, (3) below standards, and (4) academic warning. These are very rough cuts, and they tell us little about individual students' reading strengths and weaknesses. Responses to individual items are not given, so we cannot see what students may have struggled with, but we do get a sense of whom our struggling readers may be, and whom our proficient readers may be. This can serve as a starting point when we begin to consider whom we will group together for strategic reading. We cannot ascertain who may have had a terrible testing day, and who may have done better than expected. That information can only come from the work we do with students each day and the informal assessments and observations that we conduct.

Computerized assessments such as the Measures of Academic Progress (MAP) test are becoming more common in schools, and they, too, can provide us some helpful information about our students' reading. They assess different areas of reading, including fiction and nonfiction comprehension, vocabulary, language usage, and so on. Students complete this assessment on a computer, and the difficulty of questions automatically adjusts depending on how successful they are in answering initial questions. Once the assessment is complete, teachers receive scores on each subtest area in order to determine literacy strengths and weaknesses, and students also receive a Lexile score, which is a reading level, ranging from 200 to 1700 and designed to help teachers choose appropriate reading materials for each of their students. This assessment is far from perfect, yet it does give teachers a good starting place for grouping their students. We are in favor of using it for initial placement, as long as teachers remain tuned into their students and their potential for growth. We never want a number or a score to define students, though we know how easily that can happen.

It will likely be a combination of the above assessments, informal and formal, that will help teachers best understand their students and their reading strengths and needs. We imagine that teachers will observe students closely during the first weeks of school, and will also talk to their students about their reading, listen to them read aloud, ask questions about their books, read aloud to them, and observe how their students engage with stories. We also imagine that teachers will be asked to do certain reading assessments, such as fluency measures or MAP testing, and they will use that data to corroborate what they have learned from their observations. Even still, no assessment or set of assessments can give us everything we need to know. We recommend that teachers get started with strategic reading groups even if questions remain about their students. They can use all the information available to make an informed decision about reading level, reading needs, and so on—and then just plunge into strategic reading groups. The following section will assist in understanding the role and importance of ongoing assessment.

ONGOING ASSESSMENT OF STRATEGIC READING GROUPS

Assessment is ever on teachers' minds, and one of the questions that teachers often ask us is, "How do you assess students during strategic reading?" Currently in schools, teachers feel constant pressure to demonstrate the effectiveness of their teaching via student assessment. A conversation we had with teachers at a middle school led to an epiphany for all of us in that we realized that the work we do with each individual student during strategic reading groups was, in fact, an ongoing assessment of student reading.

One teacher put it this way: "So, I listen to each student from the group read individually and I help them when they have difficulty, right? Basically I'm doing a running record with each student in the group every time I meet with them. Strategic reading is like diagnostic reading."

When teachers do this kind of work with students multiple times per week, they get diagnostic information about the kinds of things students do when they read, particularly when they read material that is challenging for them. Table 8.2 provides a look at different areas of reading and the diagnostic questions that can be answered simply by listening to individual students read during strategic reading groups. This is just a sampling of the kind of information a teacher can glean. The more teachers do it, the more they find they learn about their students as readers. The answers to these questions will help guide the ongoing assessment of students and can also inform a teacher's conferences with parents. It may also assist the work of the school's intervention team and add detail to report card writing.

Every time a teacher reads with a student, the teacher learns something new about that student. The teacher also learns which strategies seem to be the most helpful in assisting that student with a challenge. If the teacher takes brief notes about students as she works with them, she will accumulate a record of students' struggles during strategic

Table 8.2   Examples of Diagnostic Questions Answered in Strategic Reading Groups

Area of Reading	Questions Answered
Student encounters unknown vocabulary word.	• Does student struggle with decoding? • Does student decode word and keep reading without trying to determine meaning? • Which strategies does student use (or fail to use) to determine meaning of word?
Student encounters text with many nonfiction features.	• Does student read through text and ignore text features? • Does student look at text features but seem unclear about how the features can help make meaning of text? • Does student use text features to help make meaning of difficult concepts?
Student demonstrates a lack of fluency marked by problems with pace, prosody, or punctuation.	• Does student notice the problem with fluency? • Is comprehension impacted? • What strategy does the teacher suggest to help student address fluency?
Student lacks background knowledge to make sense of text.	• Does student notice what he or she doesn't know? • Does student have a strategy to help connect to text? • What strategy does the teacher suggest to help student connect to text?

reading, over time, as well as the strategies she reinforced each time. Different teachers we've worked with have different ways of keeping these records. Some have a clipboard with 5 × 8 note cards, one for each student, where they take brief notes during and after each meeting. Others write on sticky notes during strategic reading and then transfer those notes into a binder, where they have sections for each student. Some teachers create their own recording forms, very similar to the one in Table 8.3, where they record the name of the student, the date they worked with the student, the title and level of the material being used, and what they worked on that day.

Over time, documents such as this provide a portrait of a reader, allowing teachers to note trends and challenges faced in reading as well as strategies used to overcome those challenges. Teachers use record keeping to annotate their work with students and to remind students of the work of previous groups. For example, we observed a teacher, Mrs. White, working with a student, Josh, in a strategic reading group who

Table 8.3   Sample Strategic Reading Record Keeping Sheet

	Student's Name: Aliya B.		
Date	*Book Title*	*Level*	*Notes*
10/12	*Black Holes and Other Space Phenomena*	T	Unable to figure out meaning of "crater." Reminded her to look at pictures and captions . . . found more about craters in a caption and she came up with workable definition.
10/15	*Lost Star: Story of Amelia Earhart*	T	Read very fluently; could answer questions. Try another T next time then may be time to move her up a level.
10/19	*A Picture of Freedom*	T	Absolutely no difficulties with this book. Great comprehension, good strategy for figuring out vocab (thought of a word that made sense). Try her in new group.
10/22	*Remember the Ladies*	V	Background knowledge lacking. Trouble understanding "striking workers." Asked her to think about current news she's heard about workers going on strike. Making that connection helped her figure out the section. Level V seems appropriate.

had trouble telling the teacher the most important thing he had just read. The teacher glanced back over her notes, and the following interaction took place:

Mrs. White: Do you remember when we read that book about volcanoes? You had trouble then coming up with the most important idea. Do you remember what you did that helped?

Josh: I went back and reread the paragraph.

Mrs. White: That's right. Let's try that again. Go back and reread this paragraph, and while you're reading, I want you to think of what the author is trying to tell you.

When teachers can help students make connections to books or materials they've read in the past, challenges they've faced, and strategies for overcoming reading challenges, students are more likely to make those connections themselves, when they read independently. Repetition and reminders of what they have done in the past can help students internalize successful reading strategies.

Changing Groups

The kinds of diagnostic records that teachers keep, as described previously, can also help teachers consider which students may no longer be appropriately placed in their group. Consider the information Mrs. White recorded about Aliya's reading in Table 8.3. Because Mrs. White kept careful records, she noticed right away when Aliya stopped having any major difficulties with the Level T selections. There are times when students do better with a certain day's text because they have an interest in the topic or lots of background knowledge about it; conversely, there may be days that a student struggles more than usual with text, possibly because of a lack of background knowledge, or maybe because of more personal issues, such as feeling ill or tired or having trouble with a friend.

While we want teachers to always notice if the material used in strategic reading groups is either too easy or too hard, we don't think teachers should move students immediately. Our advice is to see how that student does in the same level text in the next day or two to see if the trend continues. In the case of Aliya, Mrs. White kept her in Level T text over the course of the next two strategic reading groups, saw that she continued to read these texts with ease, and subsequently moved her into the next group up, which was reading Level V texts. This proved to be an appropriate move for Aliya, but Mrs. White knows to keep an eye on all kids at all times. If Aliya began to struggle again, Mrs. White would be tuned into that and would make changes as appropriate.

One of the benefits of strategic reading groups is just how flexible they are designed to be. Once we realize that students are progressing at a rate beyond their classmates in their group, we move them into more challenging texts. Similarly, when we see that certain students aren't progressing as quickly as the rest of their peers, we sometimes have to change the composition of the group. We urge teachers to take advantage of this flexibility, and to realize that group membership isn't set in stone. There is flexibility to make changes, to occasionally make mistakes, and to correct them quickly and easily. It doesn't harm a student to be erroneously placed in a group that is too easy or too hard, as long as the teacher is open to making changes after she realizes the mistake. We'd rather see this than the opposite problem, when teachers do not move students at all, in spite of evidence that demonstrates a change is necessary.

9

Managing the Rest of the Class During Strategic Reading Groups

When we do strategic reading work with teachers in preservice classes as well as during professional development at schools, one of the topics that always comes up is what to do with the rest of the class. We tell teachers that they truly can't do strategic grouping if the rest of their class is not well managed. Working with students during strategic reading groups is hard work. Teachers have to listen carefully to individual students to know when and how to provide appropriate cueing. If they are worried about what the rest of the class is doing, they will not have the attention required for the cognitively difficult task of providing appropriate and constructive cues to the students with whom they work.

We have observed in classrooms where the rest of the class has not received enough, or any, instruction in how to occupy themselves in meaningful ways during strategic reading. Though teachers are physically present with their group, their minds are almost entirely occupied by the activities of the rest of the class. Rather than intently listening to each group member read, they spend a good amount of time doing police work: snapping their fingers at someone who gets out of his seat, redirecting someone who talks too loudly to her seatmate, or telling the entire class to stay on task. When we see this happen, we tell teachers to forget strategic reading groups for a week or two, and to concentrate exclusively on teaching the class how to work independently. It's better for a teacher to lose a week of strategic reading groups than to continue doing them when not really able to focus on the group of readers.

Indeed, we never advise teachers to begin doing strategic reading immediately; rather, we recommend spending the entire first month of school teaching students the rules and procedures for engaging in successful independent literacy work.

FIRST MONTH OF SCHOOL

There are a range of literacy activities that students can do while the teacher works with a small group, and there is no one recipe for how students should spend this time. We have observed classes where the entire class engages in silent reading or independent writing while the teacher works with a strategic reading group. Other teachers have set up centers, so that two or more students work cooperatively at the vocabulary center, the computer center, or the writing center. There are many books filled with ideas for literacy-related centers for middle grades (e.g., Diller, 2005; Finney, 2003; Prevatte, 2007), and this chapter isn't about the kinds of centers teachers can use; our hope is to demonstrate the importance of dedicating a good chunk of time to explaining, modeling, and practicing procedures for successful participation in independent literacy work, no matter which activities a teacher chooses for students. (Note that the work of Boushey and Moser [2006] provides an excellent overview of how to set up procedures for independent work. Many consider their book *The Daily Five* to be for elementary teachers, but their ideas are transferable to middle grade teachers.)

The first month of school is critical for teaching students about the procedures of the classroom, including how to function during independent literacy time. No matter what teachers choose for students to do when they work with strategic reading groups, teachers need to be explicit about their expectations for this time. Say, for example, that a teacher wishes to do strategic small group reading work while the rest of her class reads independently. By middle school, she might think that this is an easy and obvious task. Students have been reading independently in class for years. She will tell them to read quietly while she works with a group, and *voila*—they will read quietly while she works with a group. In truth, though, this is rarely so simple. It is true that students who have been asked to read independently in previous years often have less trouble getting back into this habit come the beginning of a new year. However, it is also true that independent reading comes more easily for some students than others, and some students probably still haven't mastered this skill even once they arrive at middle school. In addition, group dynamics change from year to year, as do individual kids, particularly as they enter the middle school years and they become much more tuned into peers.

Teachers need to be clear in what they need from students during independent literacy time, and they need to state this explicitly at the beginning of the school year and reinforce it periodically. The next section of this chapter looks at how a teacher prepares her students to behave and work appropriately during independent reading. When appropriate, we provide the actual words a teacher might use in teaching the students. Though there are many ways to do this, this example typifies the amount of explicit detail needed to ensure students understand the entire process of reading independently. Lessons to explain procedures for independent writing, buddy reading, and word work should have the same level of detail.

Procedures for Teaching Students About Independent Literacy Work

Mrs. Lee is talking to her whole eighth-grade class. First, she sets the purpose for doing independent literacy activities:

Mrs. Lee: This year, I'm going to be working with small groups in reading. I'm going to call them strategic reading groups, because when I work with small groups, we're going to be practicing reading strategies. I will tell you a lot more about these groups soon, but in the meantime, I need to tell you how important it will be for the rest of the class to work independently and quietly. Why do you think this would be so important?

Mrs. Lee calls on a student who responds, "So that you can concentrate on the reading group?" Mrs. Lee nods her head in agreement, and goes on to tell the students how important their independent literacy work will be and how important her work with strategic reading groups will be:

Mrs. Lee: Exactly. You are middle schoolers, and you read very well. In order for me to help you become even better readers, I need to listen very carefully. I need to detect when and where you might be having difficulties and provide you with help, on the spot, so that you can become even better readers. If I have one ear on my group and one ear on the rest of the class, there's no way I can concentrate well enough to provide that kind of help. I need to know that the rest of you are working hard and not bothering anyone so that I can give 100 percent of my attention to your classmates in the strategic reading group.

The first activity we're going to work on is reading silently. Reading by yourself makes you a better reader and the more time you spend reading, the better reader you will be. So, while I'm working with small groups, you'll be getting the practice reading that will make you better readers. At first, you'll need to be able to read for 15 minutes without interrupting me or bothering anyone else. What do you think we'll need to do to make sure everyone in here can read for 15 minutes?

Students might turn and talk to come up with answers such as the following: have a good choice of books, magazines, and other good things to read; don't sit too close to people who may distract you; or pick something that interests you.

Mrs. Lee makes a chart of students' ideas. She may add her own suggestions, too. She does this to make sure that students remember these ideas over time.

Mrs. Lee: Good! This is a great list, and I will keep it posted in our room so that you can remember what you need to do to read independently without bothering anyone.

Depending on time, Mrs. Lee may continue with this lesson, or wait until the next day.

In any event, the next step would be to troubleshoot possible things that could go wrong. Mrs. Lee approaches it this way:

Mrs. Lee: So, you're sitting in a comfortable spot reading your books and I'm working with a small group right there. [gestures to a table at the back of the room] What possible things could happen to disrupt your reading?

Mrs. Lee asks students to turn and talk to a peer to come up with ideas and then share with the whole group, as the following student, Brianna, does.

Brianna: Well, someone might decide they don't like the book that they're reading.

Mrs. Lee uses this statement to reinforce previous lessons about the importance of choosing the right materials.

Mrs. Lee: That's true. It is really important that you pick something to read that you're sure you like, and also to make sure it's not too difficult for you. Don't you think it's going to be very important that you choose reading material very carefully? If you're going to have to read straight through, without stopping and without bothering anyone, then you have to put a lot of thought into picking a book or magazine that really interests you. You can't just walk over to our library, thumb through some books, and find a book with a cool cover to read during this time. Remember what we've talked about as far as choosing books. Look at the back cover and read what it says there. That's where the publisher tries to entice you into reading the book, and it gives a brief summary of the book's highlights. Then thumb through the book. If it's nonfiction, there will likely be pictures or diagrams or graphs.

See if those intrigue you. Read the first couple pages of the book. What happens? Are you drawn in and want to read more? Or do you have to force yourself just to read those pages?

She goes on to anticipate possible challenges for the students:

Another thing to think about as you read those pages is how challenging the book is. If it's too hard, you will have trouble paying attention as you read, and that's when behavior sometimes heads south. Assume that you're going to be reading completely on your own. You're not going to be able to ask me or anyone else what a word means or how to say it, so if you read the first couple pages, and there are several words you don't know, that may mean the book is too hard right now. Remember the five-finger rule. Open the book to any page and read. For every word that you can't figure out, put one finger down. If you put every finger down and you haven't gotten through even one page, that book may be too hard.

Mrs. Lee continues this lesson by asking students to create a list of what else could go wrong during their 15 minutes of reading silently. This list might include:

- Someone has to go to the bathroom.
- Someone decides he doesn't like the book he has chosen after all.
- Someone laughs too loudly.
- Someone starts talking to the person next to her.
- Someone gets restless and can't sit still.

To do this kind of lesson, it is helpful to first consider one's own comfort level. Teachers may ask themselves the following questions: Is it okay if students get up to go to the bathroom or do I need to make sure everyone has an opportunity to use the facilities prior to strategic reading groups? If I have a student or students who have a hard time sitting still for 15 minutes, am I okay with them standing or walking while they read?

Laughing (or making other noises) while reading a book can be a natural outcome of reading a particularly funny (or sad, or shocking) passage. If students really enjoy their books, it's also possible that they will come to something that they're just dying to share with someone else. Teachers should think about how they might deal with these things in class. We know teachers who have vastly different levels of tolerance for movement and noise. Some teachers we've worked with do not feel they can work with small groups while there is any noise from the rest of their class. Others purposely sit with their backs to the rest of the class and ignore minor amounts of movement or "buzz" while they work with the small group. It's important to know one's self. If someone is the type of person who gets distracted by the slightest rustling sound, then this teacher will have a different approach than a teacher who can tolerate more noise or motion, and the procedures teachers each teach their students will reflect that difference.

Certainly, middle school students are social creatures, and their need to share something with their neighbor will come up during independent literacy time. We are big fans of sticky notes during independent reading, because students can use them to mark passages that are especially funny or moving, or they can write down words that they don't know or questions they have, or parts they would like to share with someone else.

We recommend allowing students to keep a packet of sticky notes in their desks for those moments when they come to something noteworthy in their reading that they don't want to forget. After the teacher finishes with his strategic reading group, he can allow his students to turn to their friend or the person next to them to talk about what they've been reading and to share what they've written on their sticky notes. Knowing that they will have this time to turn and talk can really help students remain quiet during their 15 minutes of reading.

Choosing Something to Read

Students need to practice choosing a book or magazine or other reading material that will hold their attention for as long as possible. This is an important step. The students who tend to get distracted during silent reading are those who have picked too quickly or who have picked something too difficult. Teachers should spend some time talking to their students about the books they have chosen, particularly those students whom teachers think may be more likely to be disruptive while they're working with a reading group.

Practice

After teachers have spent a good amount of time explaining the procedures for silent reading, talking over the possible problems that could arise and potential solutions to those problems, and choosing materials to read as shown previously, it is important to devote class time to practicing. Boushey and Moser (2006) and Atwell (1998) talk about the importance of building stamina for independent literacy work. We agree that it can be unreasonable to assume that students will right away be able to read for 15 minutes straight. Rather, we can think about working up to 15 minutes of reading.

Mrs. Lee might begin a practice session as follows:

Mrs. Lee: Everyone take out the book or magazine you selected. Be sure you are comfortable and ready to read. I am going to set a timer for 15 minutes. Remember that if you are not happy with the text you selected, do as we discussed and try again. Let's see if everyone is able to read for 15 minutes, or if there may be problems that arise that make that too difficult. As soon as I notice that someone is distracted or talking, I will stop the timer, even if the 15 minutes isn't over. We'll talk about how things went after we're done reading.

Teachers should not be too disappointed if their students cannot read for 15 minutes straight the first time they practice this. Though some classes may be able to read 15 minutes without disruptions the first time, it's more likely that something will happen before the 15 minutes is through, so a teacher can just aim to read for as long as possible on the first day of practice. Like Mrs. Lee does, the teacher should let students know that she will stop them the very first time something happens (e.g., someone begins talking instead of reading), and that will become the baseline time. Each day during this practice time, the teacher will aim to build the amount of time that students can read independently, up to 15 minutes or more. Teachers often graph the class's efforts each day, so that they can show students their progress visually.

As students become accustomed to their independent literacy work, teachers will need to continue to provide support. Class meetings to reflect on students' progress can be helpful for troubleshooting. Students can consider what kind of problems arose as they practiced reading for an extended period of time, and as a group, they can brainstorm ideas for dealing with that problem in the future. (This looks much like the brainstorming with which Mrs. Lee's class engaged in the previous example.)

Though initially, teachers should aim to get students reading independently for 15 minutes, eventually students are going to need to work independently for 30 minutes, enough time for their teacher to work with two strategic reading groups. (An exception to this is if the school only offers language arts instruction during one period, with no additional time for reading instruction, in which case we recommend doing only one strategic reading group per day. See Chapter 2, Table 2.4.)

Some teachers we've worked with simply have their students continue to read silently during their second strategic reading group, and that can work just fine. Others find that some of their students need additional options in order to stay focused, and so they incorporate writing into their independent literacy work. Table 9.1 provides a look at possible activities students can engage in independently.

Regardless of what independent activities teachers decide are appropriate for their students, it is important to explain and model procedures, as Mrs. Lee did for independent reading. Troubleshooting possible problems prior to practicing activities is also advised. For example, if teachers

Table 9.1   Possible Independent Literacy Activities for Middle School Students

Activity	Short Description
Journal writing	Journals can be open-ended where students write about events in their lives or about what's on their mind, problems they're dealing with, etc. Journals can also be more directed, such as a reading response journal, where students reflect on the independent reading they've been doing, choosing from a list of questions (could be class generated) to reflect on and answer.
Partner reading	Instead of reading silently, students can read with a partner. Partners read the same book, and they can choose to take turns reading it aloud, to each other; or they can read silently, and then stop at agreed upon points to talk about what they've read so far. Teachers who allow students to partner read generally need to have a greater tolerance for ambient noise while they work with small groups.
Computer work	Depending on the availability of computers in the classroom, teachers can certainly have students work on computer based literacy activities (online learning games, story writing, online books, etc.) during independent literacy time. This is a good time to use computers that may often sit unused during the remainder of the class day.
Literacy games	There are many board games appropriate for middle grade students, including Boggle, Scrabble, Scattergories, Apples to Apples, Bananagrams, Quiddler, etc. that are wonderful for students to engage with vocabulary, word patterns, etc. Careful explanation of rules and modeling of appropriate behavior are necessary to make word games a successful addition to independent literacy activities. Teachers need to be able to tolerate the conversations and excitement inherent with these kinds of games.
Word work	Because students within any given middle school class tend to be at very different levels with regard to spelling and vocabulary, approaching word work as an independent or small group activity is a good way to meet students' needs. Students can work on word pattern sorts or vocabulary sorts, word building activities using base words and affixes, making big words (Cunningham, Hall, & Heggie, 2001), etc.

are going to ask their students to write for 15 minutes straight, students need to know what to do if they

- break a pencil or run out of paper,
- run out of things to write,
- decide they want to change topics, or
- can't spell a word.

Similarly, if students work at the computer, it is important to discuss the kinds of problems that may arise, including possible issues with taking turns, technological problems such as the computer freezing up, and so forth. It is preferable to have students consider what the potential problems will be for each of the independent literacy activities they may engage in, so they take ownership of the solutions. All of these potential problems can be posted, with possible solutions, in a prominent place in the room, for students to consult when they work independently.

For each literacy activity option, teachers should consider how to ensure that students can maintain stamina for at least 15 minutes. Just as students practiced reading independently for longer and longer periods of time, they can do the same with partner reading and writing.

Putting It All Together

Once students have learned how to engage in each literacy activity that their teacher decides to use, it is important to practice putting everything together. For example, a teacher who has decided to use independent reading and journal writing as his independent literacy activities should do some dry runs, during which he pulls a small group of kids over to the strategic reading area (a special table, a comfortable corner of the room, a group of desks pushed together) and asks the other students to practice what they would do when "real" strategic reading groups start. During this dry run, the teacher can do some informal assessments of the students he has pulled, or he could listen to them read, or he could even explain the procedures for students that are in the strategic reading group. The focus isn't on this small group, however; rather, this is a time for the teacher to observe how well the rest of the class engages in independent literacy work. After 15 minutes, if all has gone well, he can pull another group of students to the strategic reading area, and ask the rest of the class to engage in journal writing. Again, he may do some informal assessments of the students in the small group, but his focus is on the rest of the class, and how well they're handling themselves. After another 15 minutes, he can pull the class back together, discuss their progress, and do some troubleshooting if necessary. Once the class seems to be able to handle this kind of independent work, it is time to begin doing strategic reading groups.

Taking a Break Between Groups

Students of all ages react differently when asked to work independently. For some students, this is not a problem at all, and they could likely work independently for a good chunk of the school day. For others, however, working independently can be quite taxing. We have found that rather than ask students to work independently for 30 or more minutes, it is a good idea to take a 5-minute break in between strategic reading groups.

Table 9.2 One Way to Schedule Strategic Reading Time

Time	Strategic Reading	Independent Literacy Activities
9–9:15 a.m.	Teacher works with Group 1.	The rest of the class reads silently.
9:15–9:20	*Short break: Turn and talk to the person or people around you and tell them one thing you really like (or don't like) about the book you are reading.*	
9:20–9:35	Teacher works with Group 2.	The rest of the class writes about their reading in their literature response journals.
9:35–9:40	*Short meeting for students and teacher to check in about independent work and how things went. (This meeting time can be dropped once things are in full swing.)*	

During this time, students can turn and talk to their classmates about the book they've just been reading, or share the writing they've been doing. Or, the teacher could use the 5 minutes to read a poem or chapter from the book she's been reading aloud. Then, the teacher refocuses the class on the next independent activity and gets back to work with the next strategic reading group.

We recommend taking things slowly once teachers get started with strategic reading groups. If a teacher is not used to asking students to work independently, it may be better initially to aim for doing one strategic reading group per day. This allows time for both the teacher and the students to get used to this kind of work. At first, the teacher may also want to do a daily "check-in" with the class to get their feedback about the independent literacy work they did. This could be their time to continue to troubleshoot procedures and behavior, while the teacher gets accustomed to working with a small group and letting go of total control of the class. Once students and teacher feel comfortable with one strategic reading group per day, teachers can add the second group.

Class at a Glance

Tables 9.2 and 9.3 offer two options for how teachers can organize their classrooms during independent literacy work. These schedules are for those teachers who are able to meet with two strategic reading groups, two or three times per week. Teachers in schools that have shorter periods of time for literacy instruction would only work with one group per day, and would adjust accordingly. (Chapter 2, Tables 2.2, 2.3, and 2.4 provide a look at different configurations of the literacy block.)

Table 9.3   Alternate Schedule for Strategic Reading Time

Time	Strategic Reading	Independent Literacy Activities
9–9:15	Teacher works with Group 1.	Class works in centers: computer center vocabulary center writing center classroom library
9–9:20	Short break: Teacher checks in with center groups for a progress report.	
9:20–9:35	Teacher works with Group 2.	Groups rotate so that they're at a different center than previously.
9:35–9:40	Short meeting for students and teacher to check in about independent work and how things went. (This meeting time can be dropped once things are in full swing.)	

MONITORING AND ASSESSING INDEPENDENT LITERACY WORK

We feel strongly that the work that students do independently while their teacher works with small groups should be productive and should contribute to students becoming stronger and more independent readers and writers. This should not just be busywork designed to keep students quiet. That being said, we do not feel that teachers should spend too much time assessing the work that students do during this time. If students read independently during strategic reading groups, then providing time for them to turn and talk to their classmates about their reading is one way to show them that they are being held accountable for their reading without formal assessment.

Some teachers we know reserve one day a week or every other week for students to report back to the class about the independent literacy work they've been doing. This is a great time for them to share a new book or read a paragraph or two from a piece they've been writing. They may also talk about the games they've been playing or the words they've been learning. We feel that this kind of informal monitoring is quite motivating for students; knowing that they will have a chance to share what they've been doing helps to ensure that they will work productively during independent work.

One final note is that student literacy learning should be viewed holistically. Students get better at reading and writing by doing a variety of things like those described previously. It is not necessary to track every nuance of student learning, but rather to be sure that the overall classroom literacy experience results in acceleration of student achievement.

Afterword

As we explained in Chapter 1, we designed strategic reading groups as scaffolds for new, urban teachers who struggled with the logistical issues related to small group instruction. It seemed logical to us that the first step was to reduce the amount of time spent in the groups, as this was certainly the most obvious way to attend to some of the management issues the teachers were experiencing. It was our goal to cut as much of the fat out of these groups as possible, to shift any instruction that could be done whole group to a whole group context, and focus on what was absolutely necessary instruction within the small group.

We knew that the individual interaction between teacher and student was a priority, and we designed our groups to highlight this most important component. We assumed that once teachers got these groups tighter and their classroom management improved, they could go back to what we had observed to be more typical small group work, with a focus on before-, during-, and after-reading strategies that the teacher felt was suited for the particular group in front of him.

However, we became more and more moved by the simple act of student reading to teacher, and the interactions that resulted. We realized that instruction needed to remain on the spot and designed to address individual student needs, and that generalized reading strategies were more appropriately taught whole group. It is now our belief that no matter the experience level of the teacher, this is the most productive use of small group time. The teachers we have worked with echo this belief. They describe relationships they've developed with students that they hadn't had before, and that they hadn't expected to form during strategic reading groups. They tell us that their students look forward to strategic reading groups, and they miss them if they are canceled due to an assembly or other class disruption. Teachers report knowing more about their students' reading than ever before.

We spend time in middle school classrooms modeling strategic reading groups for teachers with their students. Most often, we have a large number of adults observing the groups. Each and every time, we have a moment of panic: "What if it doesn't work? What if I have nothing to say with all these people watching me?" But each and every time it becomes more and more clear that strategic reading groups are consistently effective. We always learn something about the students we listen to, and we are always amazed at what can get done in the course of 2 minutes.

We encourage teachers to dive in and try this practice. At first, it may feel awkward, but our coaching of dozens of teachers has shown us that in fairly short order it becomes an important piece of excellent literacy instruction.

References

Andersen, H. C. (1983). *The complete fairy tales and stories.* New York: Anchor Books.

Anderson, S. (2011, March 6). What I really want is someone rolling around in the text. *New York Times*, p. MM46.

Atwell, N. (1998). *In the middle: New understandings about writing, reading, and learning.* Portsmouth, NH: Boynton-Cook.

Berne, J., & Degener, S. (2010) *Responsive guided reading in Grades K–5: Simplifying small group instruction.* New York: Guilford Press.

Blanton, W. E., Wood, K. D., & Taylor, B. (2010). Rethinking middle school reading instruction: A basic literacy activity. In M. Cappello & B. Moss (Eds.), *Contemporary readings in literacy education* (pp. 213–222). Thousand Oaks, CA: Sage.

Boushey, G., & Moser, J. (2006). *The daily five.* York, ME: Stenhouse.

Boyle, M. (2011). *Analysis of the relationship between narrative and informational text reading as part of the development of the STEP primary literacy assessment.* Manuscript submitted for publication.

Brown, B. (2011, May 9). Alexander the Great. *Junior Scholastic*, 20–22.

Bryson, B. (2000). *In a sun-burned country.* New York: Broadway Books.

Chall, J. S., Jacobs, V., & Baldwin, L. (1990). *The reading crisis: Why poor children fall behind.* Cambridge, MA: Harvard University Press.

Christopher, M. (2008). *On the court with . . . LeBron James.* New York: Little Brown and Company.

Clay, M. M. (2000). *Running records for classroom teachers.* Portsmouth, NH: Heinemann.

Clay, M. M. (2006). *An observation survey of early literacy achievement* (2nd ed.). Portsmouth, NH: Heinemann.

Cranford, L. (1996). *The bridge.* Retrieved from www.jhedge.com/story/fiction/bridge.htm

Cullinan, B.E. (2000). Independent reading and school achievement. *School Library Media Research, 3.* Retrieved from www.ala.org/ala/mgrps/divs/aasl/aaslpubsandjournals/slmrb/slmrcontents/volume32000/independent.cfm

Cunningham, P., Hall, D., & Heggie, T. (2001). *Making big words, Grades 3–6: Multilevel, hands-on spelling and phonics activities.* Grand Rapids, MI: Frank Schaffer.

Daniels, H. A. (1990). Young writers and readers reach out: Developing a sense of audience. In T. Shanahan (Ed.), *Reading and writing together: New perspectives for the classroom* (pp. 99–129). Norwood, MA: Christopher-Gordon.

Diller, D. (2005). *Practice with purpose: Literacy work stations for Grades 3–6.* York, ME: Stenhouse.

Dorn, L., French, C., & Jones, T. (1998). *Apprenticeship in learning: Transitions across reading and writing.* Portland, ME: Stenhouse.

Duke, N. K., & Pearson, P. D. (2002). Effective practices for developing reading comprehension. In A. E. Farstrup & S. J. Samuels (Eds.), *What research has to say about reading instruction* (3rd ed., pp. 205–242). Newark, DE: International Reading Association.

Durkin, D. (1993). *Teaching them to read* (6th ed.). Boston: Allyn & Bacon.

Facklam, M. (1992). Dancing bees. In M. Facklam (Ed.), *Bees dance and whales sing: The mysteries of animal communication* (pp. 13–17). San Francisco: Sierra Club Books.

FEMA. (2010). *The national flood insurance program.* Retrieved from www.fema.gov/plan/prevent/floodplain/index.shtm

Finney, S. (2003). *Independent reading activities that keep kids learning . . . while you teach small groups.* New York: Scholastic.

Fountas, I. C., & Pinnell, G. S. (1996). *Guided reading: Good first teaching for all children.* Portsmouth, NH: Heinemann.

Goodman, L. (2011, April). Fighting with purpose: Veteran Paul Chappell on the need to end war. *The Sun,* 4–8.

Harness, C. (2003). *Remember the ladies: 100 great American women.* New York: Scholastic.

Jackson, S. (1992). *The lottery and other stories.* New York: Noonday Press.

Lauber, P. (1990). *Lost star: The story of Amelia Earhart.* New York: Scholastic.

Macaulay, D. (1998). *The new way things work.* New York: Houghton Mifflin.

McKissack, P. (2003). *A picture of freedom: The diary of Clotee, a slave girl, Belmont Plantation, Virginia 1859.* New York: Scholastic.

Miller, K., & Levine, J. (2010). *Biology.* New York: Prentice Hall.

NutritionData.com. (n.d.). *Glycemic index.* Retrieved from http://nutritiondata.self.com/topics/glycemic-index

Opitz, M. F., & Ford, M. P. (2001). *Reaching readers: Flexible and innovative strategies for guided reading.* Portsmouth, NH: Heinemann.

Paulsen, G. (1987). *Hatchet.* New York: Simon and Schuster Books for Young Readers.

Prevatte, L. (2007). *Middle school literacy centers: Connecting struggling students to literature.* Gainesville, FL: Maupin House.

Ravitch, D. (2011, March 20). *Obama's war on schools.* Retrieved from www.thedailybeast.com/newsweek/2011/03/20/obama-s-war-on-schools.html

Samuels, S.J. (2006). Toward a model of reading fluency. In S. J. Samuels & A. E. Fastrup (Eds.), *What research has to say about fluency instruction* (pp. 24–46). Newark, DE: International Reading Association.

Shea, M. (2006). *Where's the glitch? How to use running records with older readers, Grades 5–8.* Portsmouth, NH: Heinemann.

Silverstein, A., Silverstein, V., & Nunn, L. (1999). *Cuts, scrapes, scabs, and scars.* New York: Scholastic.

Steele, P. (1998). *Black holes and other space phenomena.* New York: Scholastic.

Sundby, S. (2000). *Cut down to size at high noon: A math adventure.* Watertown, MA: Charlesbridge Publishing.

The search for life in outer space. (n.d.). Retrieved from www.astrocentral.co.uk /life.html

van den Broek, P., & Kremer, K. (2000). The mind in action: What it means to comprehend during reading. In B. M. Taylor, M. F. Graves, & P. van den Broek (Eds.), *Reading for meaning: Fostering comprehension in the middle grades* (pp. 1–31). Newark, DE: International Reading Association.

Verne, J. (1995). *20,000 leagues under the sea.* New York: Tom Doherty Associates.

Vygotsky, L. S. (1978). *Mind and society: The development of higher mental processes.* Cambridge, MA: Harvard University Press.

Wilkinson, I. A .G., & Anderson, R. C. (1995). Sociocognitive processes in guided silent reading: A microanalysis of small-group lessons. *Reading Research Quarterly, 30,* 710–740.

Index

CORWIN
A SAGE Company

The Corwin logo—a raven striding across an open book—represents the union of courage and learning. Corwin is committed to improving education for all learners by publishing books and other professional development resources for those serving the field of PreK–12 education. By providing practical, hands-on materials, Corwin continues to carry out the promise of its motto: **"Helping Educators Do Their Work Better."**